ABRAHAM
THE LORD WILL PROVIDE

ABRAHAM
THE LORD WILL PROVIDE

EDWARD G. DOBSON

Fleming H. Revell
A Division of Baker Book House
Grand Rapids, Michigan 49516

Published by Fleming H. Revell
A Division of Baker Book House
P. O. Box 6287
Grand Rapids, MI 49516-6287
Printed in the United States of America

Library of Congress Cataloging-in-Publication Data

Dobson, Ed.
    Abraham : the Lord will provide / Edward G. Dobson.
      p. cm.
    ISBN 0-8007-1668-X
    1. Abraham (Biblical patriarch). 2. Patriarchs (Bible)—Biography. 3. Christian life—1960. 4. Dobson, Ed. I. Title.
BS580.A3D58   1993
222'.11092—dc20
                                               92-31854

All Scripture quotations, unless otherwise indicated, are taken from the HOLY BIBLE, NEW INTERNATIONAL VERSION®. Copyright © 1973, 1978, 1984 by International Bible Society. Used by permission of Zondervan Publishing House. All rights reserved.

Scripture quotations identified AMP are from the Amplified Bible, Old Testament, copyright 1965, 1987 by the Zondervan Corporation. Used by permission.

Scripture quotations identified KJV are from the King James Version of the Bible.

The following people have granted permission to use their material:

Got Any Rivers by Oscar C. Eliason copyright © 1945 Singspiration Music/ASCAP. All rights reserved. Used by permission of Benson Music Group, Inc.

He Is Able by Paul E. Paino.

To Calvin and Eileen Dobson,
my parents, who taught
me a love for the
Word of God

Contents

Chapter One

God,
You Want Me to Do What?

By Faith . . . Abraham

Abraham—or Abram, as he is first called—is a unique individual. He is one of the most prominent figures in the entire Bible. His name occurs 308 times: 234 times in the Old Testament and 74 in the New Testament. That's a lot of references to one man. Sometimes he is a person of great faith; at other times he is a miserable failure, filled with doubt about God and himself. However, the Bible provides us with at least three distinctive descriptions of this man.

Abraham Was Called God's Friend

And the scripture was fulfilled that says, "Abraham believed God, and it was credited to him as righteousness," and he was called God's friend.

James 2:23

I'd like to be able to title my autobiography *Ed Dobson: God's Friend*. What a consuming objective. But I hesitate to make that claim.

It is one thing to say, "God is my friend," and quite another matter to claim, "I am God's friend." Since God inspired the text of the Bible, he is saying, "Abraham, you're my friend." Abraham is the only person in the Bible who carries this designation.

I wouldn't mind having a tombstone that reads:

Ed Dobson

Born, December 30, 1949

Died, _____

God's Friend

Abraham Is the Father of All Who Believe

> And he received the sign of circumcision, a seal of the righteousness that he had by faith while he was still uncircumcised. So then, he is the father of all who believe but have not been circumcised, in order that righteousness might be credited to them. And he is also the father of the circumcised who not only are circumcised but who also walk in the footsteps of the faith that our father Abraham had before he was circumcised.
>
> Romans 4:11, 12

The Scriptures tell us that Abraham is the father of both the circumcised who believe (the Jews) and the uncircumcised (the Gentiles) who believe. Abraham is the father of *all* believers.

Dispensationalists often read the promises to Abraham (Genesis 12:1–3) as uniquely Jewish in character. However, the promises conclude with a powerful statement: "And all peoples on the earth will be blessed through you." God's purpose was not only to bring a nation from Abraham and to give them a land; it was also to bless all the peoples of the earth. God had the Gentiles in mind when he forged his covenant with Abraham.

Abraham Is a Figure of True Faith

Sometimes we muddy our understanding of faith by complex theological definitions and arguments. We confine our thinking to dusty books and ivory-tower discussions.

But faith is best understood in flesh and blood—not print and paper. Abraham's life is a case study in faith and doubt. Getting into his situation, feeling his pain, seeing his doubt, understanding his thinking, we discover the real stuff of faith.

Hebrews gives us a synoptic overview of his life. Notice the emphasis on faith:

> By *faith* Abraham, even though he was past age—and Sarah herself was barren—was enabled to become a father because he considered him faithful who had made the promise. And so from this one man, and he as good as dead, came descendants as numerous as the stars in the sky and as countless as the sand on the seashore.
>
> By *faith* Abraham, when God tested him, offered Isaac as a sacrifice. He who had received the promises was about to sacrifice his one and only son, even though God had said to him, "It is through Isaac that your offspring will be reckoned." Abraham reasoned that God could raise the dead, and figuratively speaking, he did receive Isaac back from death.
>
> Hebrews 11:11, 12, 17–19

Abraham was the friend of God.
Abraham is the father of believers.
Abraham is a figure of faith.

The First Step of Faith Is the Toughest

When I was in college, I participated in many plays.

Acting is a little like preaching, with one major difference. When you act, you memorize lines, and it's tough to ad-lib. If you do, you can mess the whole thing up. When you preach, you have liberty to ad-lib—and most people don't know. When I was in plays, I always feared my mind would go blank, and I'd freeze. I would wait offstage, with my heart pumping. The first step into the spotlight in the darkened auditorium was always the hardest. After the first line I was okay.

Faith is like that. The first step into the spotlight feels intimidating. Abram took an incredible first step.

> Terah took his son Abram, his grandson Lot son of Haran, and his daughter-in-law Sarai, the wife of his son Abram, and together they set out for Ur of the Chaldeans to go to Canaan. But when they came to Haran, they settled there. Terah lived 205 years, and he died. The LORD had said to Abram, "Leave your country, your people and your father's household and go to the land I will show you."
>
> Genesis 11:31–12:1

Ur was a very famous city. If you were to leave Baghdad, Iraq, and travel to the Persian Gulf, halfway between Baghdad and the gulf you'd find the ancient Ur. It was a very prominent city, surrounded by a series of thirty-foot walls.

Back in the 1920s and 1930s, archaeologists excavated Ur and discovered royal tombs dating 2,500 years before Christ. Those tombs held musical instruments, precious jewels, and statues—all indicative of a highly sophisticated culture. In the center of the city, they discovered a temple to the moon god, Nana. It was a massive, three-layered building that reached high into the sky. At the top the people worshiped this god.

We can safely assume that Abram and his family worshiped Nana. In fact, Scripture strongly indicates this:

> Joshua said to all the people, "This is what the LORD, the God of Israel, says: 'Long ago your forefathers, including Terah the

father of Abraham and Nahor, lived beyond the River and worshiped other gods.'"

Joshua 24:2

God speaks to Abram and makes a strange and bizarre request.
In Genesis 12:1–3

Leave:
1. Your country.
2. Your people.
3. Your father's household.

I Will:
1. Show you a land.
2. Make you into a great nation.
3. Bless you.
4. Make your name great.
5. Bless those who bless you.

While the call of God may be different for us, the underlying
principle of the call is the same. First he calls us to leave our
pagan idols behind and follow him. This radical step of faith
brings the blessing of God: "I will bless you!"

For they themselves report what kind of reception you gave
us. They tell how you *turned to God from idols* to serve the living
and true God, and to wait for his Son from heaven, whom he
raised from the dead—Jesus, who rescues us from the coming
wrath.

1 Thessalonians 1:9, 10, *italics added*

Of late the evangelical faith has become rather polluted. In some
circles it demands little. The offer of faith is just another thing to
add to your life, its cost is ignored. That does not agree with the

Bible's description. Faith cost Abram his financial security, his reputation, his family relationships, and his cultural identity.

What if God's call demanded that today you:

Sell your business.
Move your family.
Forsake your reputation.

Would you follow him?

Faith and Obedience: Inseparable Entities

Terah took his son Abram, his grandson Lot son of Haran, and his daughter-in-law Sarai, the wife of his son Abram, and together they set out from Ur of the Chaldeans to go to Canaan. But when they came to Haran, they settled there.

Terah lived 205 years, and he died in Haran.

Genesis 11:31, 32

There were two major travel routes from Ur to Canaan. One went directly west across the desert; it was a difficult and hazardous course. The second went directly north along the Euphrates River to Haran and then west and south to Canaan. Abram chooses this route but makes it only to Haran. After Terah dies, God reminds Abram to go the rest of the way.

So Abram left, as the LORD had told him; and Lot went with him. Abram was seventy-five years old when he set out from Haran. He took his wife Sarai, his nephew Lot, all the possessions they had accumulated and the people they had acquired in Haran, and they set out for the land of Canaan, and they arrived there.

Genesis 12:4, 5

Faith means taking God at his word and obeying him. That's what it means to trust God. The text says, "Abram left. . . . They arrived there." Notice that his obedience was threefold:

1. *It was immediate.* He didn't spend another decade in Haran. He immediately responded to the voice of God and traveled to Canaan.
2. *His obedience was inclusive.* He took everybody with him.
3. *His obedience was complete.* "And they arrived there."

Now that's the kind of obedience that God wants in our lives.

He wants us to take him at his word and obey him—immediately, inclusively, and completely. This is how Abraham's faith is described in Hebrews 11: "By faith Abraham, when called to go to a place he would later receive as his inheritance, *obeyed* and *went*, even though he did not know where he was going" (Hebrews 11:8, *italics added*).

Let's translate this into the twentieth century. God comes to Ed Dobson and he says, "All right, Ed, I want you to leave your job; I want you to leave all your relatives; I want you to take your security and your culture and follow me. Leave everything behind, because I have something better for you."

"Well, where am I going, God?"

"That's up to me," God says.

I can't even comprehend this. At least the Lord could have sent Abram a AAA "Trip Tik" that pointed out all the beautiful spots on the way, and told Abram where he was going and what he was doing. God said, "Abram, go!" And Abram obeyed and went!

Do you know what faith is? It is taking God at his word and obeying him. Until I have obeyed, I have not really trusted him. When I do not obey God, I'm saying, "God, I really don't trust you. I really don't trust your word. I know what you have said, but

I'm going to do differently." Essentially I'm saying, "God, I don't trust you, and I don't trust your word." The hymn writer says:

> When we walk with the Lord
> In the light of His Word,
> What a glory He sheds on our way!
> While we do His good will
> He abides with us still,
> And with all who will trust and obey.
>
> Trust and obey—
> For there's no other way
> To be happy in Jesus
> But to trust and obey.
>
> JOHN H. SAMMIS

> Abraham obeyed
> Immediately
> Inclusively
> Completely

He went; he took everybody with him; he arrived.

When God Blesses—Build an Altar

Abram traveled through the land as far as the site of the great tree of Moreh at Shechem. At that time the Canaanites were in the land. The LORD appeared to Abram and said, "To your offspring I will give this land." So he built an altar there to the LORD, who had appeared to him.

Genesis 12:6, 7

God leads us by his word and confirms his leadership with his presence. The Bible says, "The LORD appeared to Abram." This is the first recorded appearance of God to a human being since

Adam and Eve. When Adam and Eve fell into sin, God put them out of the garden. They were driven from God's presence. God now appears again to a human being. He tells Abram to build an altar.

When God moves into your life in a supernatural moment like conversion or God intervenes in a special way in answer to prayer, build an altar. Do something that reminds you of his presence. Write in the front of your Bible what God did. "On this day, I trusted Christ as my Savior." Or if God met a special answer to prayer, write it down! Build altars to the presence of God. You know why? Because down the road, when you face difficult circumstances and you don't know where to turn, you can go back to your altars and recount the presence and the intervention of God. I've discovered in my own life that looking back in this way increases my faith for the crises that I face.

I have a Bethel altar hanging in the living room of our home. It's a picture of a little country church, the prayer chapel at the center of Liberty University. Before I came to Calvary Church, I went there every day for thirty minutes to pray about my future. I just felt in my heart that God was going to move our family. So for nine months, I slipped out of my office every day, walked across a little courtyard, and knelt at the front pew of the prayer chapel. I kept a diary of what God was doing in my life, what God was teaching me in his Word, and how God was leading me.

Today, when I walk into the living room of our house, there's the altar. There is no question in my mind of God's leadership. That little chapel reminds me that the same God who led Abraham is the very same God who is alive today—the same God who walks with us and is capable of meeting our every need.

We have established some Bethel altars in our church. On the last Sunday of a series of sermons on prayer, we distributed silk roses to every member of the congregation. The rose represents a prayer request—either personal or for someone else. When God answers the prayer, the people return the rose with a note telling what God did. We print the answers to prayer in the bulletin, and we put the roses in a wreath located in the sanctuary. We gave away over 4,000 roses, and it's exciting to see what God is doing.

It is with great joy that I return this rose. My prayer to find my firstborn daughter has been answered. I am a birth mother. A birth mother is a woman who gives birth to a child and relinquishes that child to another to raise, to love, to share the good and bad times, to send off to kindergarten, and to watch graduate from high school.

"For you created my inmost being; you knit me together in my mother's womb. I praise you because I am fearfully and wonderfully made; your works are wonderful, I know that full well. My frame was not hidden from you when I was made in the secret place . . ." (Psalm 139:13–15). For years my daughter's birth was secret, as was her existence. However, through a series of tragic events in my family, beginning with the death of my mother, I began to deal for the first time with this long-suppressed secret. The desire to find my child and to be given a chance to love and know her kept growing so that finally I could suppress it no longer. In May of 1990, I started to search for my daughter, born 32 years ago to me, when I was but a 15-year-old girl child. On December 24 I was given her name, Marcia, and her phone number. On December 26 I spoke with her for the very first time. It was wonderful to hear her voice, to talk to her, and to plan a reunion. What joy!

Through the years my only regular prayer was for her salvation. God is so good. Marcia was raised by a godly woman named Betty, who has since died. Marcia asked Jesus "into her heart" when she was six years old. How can I thank or praise God enough?

Our reunion went very well. With the Lord's direction we will grow closer and become more intimate as the relationship progresses. Joel 2:25–26 says, "I will repay you for the years the locust's have eaten . . . never again will my people be shamed." I have this promise to claim for the future.

As the Lord brought this very painful and buried truth to the surface of my life I was very fearful of the reality of facing it. "Now my heart is troubled, and what shall I say? 'Father, save me from this hour'? No, it was for this very reason I came to this hour. Father, glorify your name!" (John 12:27, 28). The Lord has required my faith step by step. As Lazarus took off his grave clothes and was set free to walk in newness of life, so I have been set free as each layer of my grave clothes were peeled off. It was difficult to first face my husband with this truth and to then share this with my daughters who were raised in my home. How could they ever understand or accept this? Yet they did. Their love and support have been an added blessing to me. Now I face the last step of coming out of my closet by adding to the view of my friends and others of you I love this long hidden dimension of myself. My prayer is that among my Christian brothers and sisters I will find compassion and love.

It has been years since I first accepted Christ as my Savior, and now for the first time I truly understand what that full forgiveness means and have been able to now forgive myself for the past that is irretrievable. "Forgetting what is behind and straining toward what is ahead." Because of this great forgiveness through Christ, which freed me from my past, soon I will be able to stand before you with confidence, having realized fully for the first time who I am in Christ. May God open your hearts to both my daughter and me as God grants me the courage to take this next step of faith for, "There is a time for everything, and a season for every activity under heaven: a time to be born . . . a time to search . . . a time to be silent and a time to speak . . . He has made everything beautiful in its time" (Ecclesiastes 3:1, 2, 6, 7, 11).

My prayer was answered when we found a home to move into in the Lansing area. We had two days in which to find one. Praise God!

My answer to my specific prayer is so amazing that it's hard to write it in three short lines. 1. My specific need was to know God's will regarding a job offer and if it would be beneficial to my future. I had to give them an answer by Monday, so I had to give God a time limit—but I knew he'd answer my prayer. 2. My answer wasn't as obvious as I'd hoped, but I felt my answer was to stay where I was. 3. Tuesday afternoon I received a phone call, and I was again referred to another company. I went on an interview, and this job was more than I ever dreamed of or asked from God. On Friday I got the job!

On November 7, David had brain surgery. Now, only two weeks later, we are amazed at his recovery to this point. God has miraculously acted in his and our behalf, and we are truly thankful. David still has a long way to go, but we know that God is able.

My mom's cousin was in the hospital for a long time. His name is Doug VanderLaan. He has leukemia cancer. I am happy that he can be with his family at home. The reason why I brought my rose back is because my prayers were answered. I prayed that he would be able to go home from the hospital. My grandpa helped me write this note.

A couple of weeks ago at church someone took my new coat. We prayed they would return it, and the next day my mom called church, and it was there.

I am returning my rose today because my prayer request was to have my son, Kyle, accept Jesus into his heart. On November 18, 1990 Kyle did just that. Now I get to spend eternity with him! Praise God!

Prayer

Father, I want to be called your friend. Teach me today to trust and obey. Teach me to follow you. When I step into the spotlight and the odds are overwhelming, remind me that you go with me. Reveal to me the pagan idols that hold me in bondage to the world. Show me areas in my life where I have failed to obey you immediately and completely. And God, please bless me.

Chapter Two

Is There Life Beyond the Mess?

Have you ever made a mess of your life? I don't mean, have you ever gotten into a mess? Sometimes the circumstances and problems of our life lie beyond our control, and we end up in a mess because we can't avoid it. But have you ever personally messed up your own life? Maybe you are smiling or enjoying this question. I think you know what I am talking about.

I recall a time when I was in graduate school, and I was working to pay the bills. I got a job with an interior decorator, William Key Interiors, one of the most exclusive decorating companies in South Carolina. We did not decorate homes, we decorated estates. It was one of the ultimate status symbols in South Carolina to have your home decorated by William Key Interiors.

I started out as a delivery boy and then was promoted to a cornice maker. Eventually, before I left, I did a little bit of decorating. When you are just a delivery boy, and you're delivering to these fancy estates, everybody thinks that you know something about interior decorating. I remember one of my earliest experiences.

Dennis, my boss, and I were delivering a whole bedroom full of furniture to this massive estate. We knew nothing about decorating. We were making minimum wage, delivering furniture. We pulled up to this big estate and carted all the furniture inside. I remember we had a long dresser and a short dresser. One went on one wall and the other went on the parallel wall. We had a beautiful, antique, gold-leaf mirror. Dennis said, "Ed, you hang the mirror." So I stood there, looking at the short dresser and the long dresser, thinking, *Where does the mirror go?* It made sense to me to hang it over the short dresser. So I got out the toolbox, drilled a hole in the wall, in the right position, and knocked in the plastic plug. I got the special hook for a heavy mirror and hung the thing on the wall—perfectly centered.

I was standing back, admiring my work, when the lady of the house walked in. When she saw where the mirror was hanging, she gasped. "The mirror belongs on that wall over the long dresser," she said.

"No problem, ma'am, we'll move it," I answered. So after the lady left, I took the mirror off the wall, drilled another hole in the parallel wall, stuck the plastic plug in, got the hook and hung the mirror. Then I turned and looked around this beautiful bedroom filled with expensive furniture. Right above the short dresser, about three-and-one-half feet above the center, was a plastic plug and a hole in the wall.

So the lady came in and asked, "What are you going to do about the hole?"

"Oh, no problem, ma'am, we know how to fix these things."

So she left, and I demanded, "Dennis, how *do* we fix these things?"

He said, "Well, we have a kit down in the van. . . . You know, when you bump furniture and nobody's looking, you just paint it over and kind of smooth it out."

So I got out all this plastic stuff. I pulled the plug out of the wall. I put the putty in the wall; I smoothed it over and then got out the box of paints. I know nothing about mixing paint! So I kept mixing it and mixing it until I got what I thought was close to the color.

By this time the lady was pretty ripped. I had drilled a hole in the wrong wall. There was nothing to cover it. So I started painting.

The lady was standing right over my shoulder. Finally, she pointed out, "Doesn't quite match!"

"Oh, don't worry about that, ma'am, when it dries it will be fine. You see, it's just a little bit wet, and it's kind of off, but when it dries, it will be. . . ."

"Oh, yes, I never thought of that," she said. "Thank you."

We went out and got in the truck and laughed. We got so wound up about what we had done, we backed the van into a tree! We were not interior decorators, we were interior "wreckorators." I'll never forget the pressure of trying to dig my way out of a bad situation and the terrible feeling of digging the hole deeper and deeper. (By the way, my painting didn't work. We had to redo every wall in the bedroom).

I Can Work It Out on My Own

The story of Abram's journey into Egypt is a story of a personally engineered failure. He made a mess of his whole life.

> Now there was a famine in the land, and Abram went down to Egypt to live there for a while because the famine was severe.
>
> Genesis 12:10

Abram has followed God all the way to Canaan. Great! Now he faces a famine in the land and assumes he can resolve this problem on his own. Launching out on his own, Abram goes from good, to not so good, to bad, to worse, to awful. He digs a hole so deep he cannot get out without God's help. And it all began with these failures on Abram's part.

He Failed to Trust God

In the last chapter we studied the call of Abram. God said, "Leave your country; leave your kindred; leave your family, and go to a land that I will show you, and I'll give it to you. But you must leave everything, and trust me." Abram trusted God for over 1,000 miles. He followed. He left behind his culture, his friends, and his possessions. He traveled to a country where he had never been. Then he got there and a famine hit the land. What did he do? He turned about and went to Egypt and tried to solve his own problems.

The man who trusted God for the ultimate—his future—was unwilling to trust God for the immediate—food. It doesn't make sense! The guy trusted God for the big things of life, but messed up when it came to smaller things.

Faith means trusting God for the big things as well as the little things. You know, that's where we often fail. We trust God with our souls—it's called salvation. Then we worry about the struggle we're going through and the decisions we have to make. We trust God with the ultimate: eternity! But we can't trust him to get through today?

Famines were not uncommon in Palestine. It was part of living there. Yet Abram failed to trust God and tried to solve the problem on his own. In reality it was not his problem anyway. God led him to Palestine. God would take care of him.

He Failed to Obey God

In the first nine verses of chapter 12, Abram is the man of faith. The Lord is central to every choice and move.

"The Lord had said to Abram . . . "(v. 1).
"So Abram left, as the Lord had told him . . . "(v. 4).
"The Lord appeared to Abram . . ." (v. 7).

"There he built an altar to the Lord and called on the name of the Lord" (v. 8).

In verse 10 and following, Abram is the man of failure. The contrast is striking: "Now there was a famine in the land, and Abram went down to Egypt to live there for a while because the famine was severe" (v. 10). The name of the Lord does not even appear in this verse. Abram doesn't ask. He doesn't pray. He doesn't go to Bethel. He doesn't build an altar. He doesn't seek the guidance of the Lord. Abram moves on his own initiative to solve his own problem, apart from God. We will absolutely mess up our lives when we start to move in the arm of the flesh, without the guidance of the Lord—just like Abram.

In the Old Testament, Egypt often represents human effort as opposed to divine help:

> Woe to those who go down to Egypt for help, who rely on horses, who trust in the multitude of their chariots and in the great strength of their horsemen, but do not look to the Holy One of Israel, or seek help from the LORD. Yet he too is wise and can bring disaster; he does not take back his words. He will rise up against the house of the wicked, against those who help evildoers. But the Egyptians are men and not God; their horses are flesh and not spirit. When the LORD stretches out his hand, he who helps will stumble, he who is helped will fall; both will perish together.
>
> Isaiah 31:1–3

Truman Dollar, one of my closest friends, serves as one of my accountability partners. He told me that there are three important principles to remember when you encounter problems in the church:

1. It is never as good as it seems.

2. It is never as bad as it seems.
3. The greatest myth of all is that you have taken care of the problem.

Abram struggled with all three principles.

1. Egypt was not as good as it seemed.
2. The famine in Palestine was not as bad as it seemed.
3. When he left to go to Egypt, he thought the problem was solved.

He Failed to Fear God

As he was about to enter Egypt, he said to his wife Sarai, "I know what a beautiful woman you are. When the Egyptians see you, they will say, 'This is his wife.' Then they will kill me but will let you live. Say you are my sister, so that I will be treated well for your sake and my life will be spared because of you."

Genesis 12:11–13

Abram was more afraid of the Egyptians than he was of God. He failed to fear God.

Before we get too hard on Abram, think about his ingenious plan. You see, there is more to the plan than meets the eye. Abram understood the laws of ancient Egypt. Law number one: when you're a foreigner in Egypt, and an Egyptian wants to marry your wife, he is allowed to kill you and marry your wife.

Abram was a pretty smart guy. He said to Sarai "You're beautiful. The Egyptians are going to like you. They know you are my wife. If they want to marry you, they will kill me." This was the rule of the supreme court of Egypt.

Abram came up with a great solution: "Say you're my sister." Now that was not a total lie. Abram and his wife Sarai had the same father but different mothers. So Abram's pretty slick. He's not really lying; it's just a half-truth. He also knows the marriage laws of Egypt. If you want to marry someone, you must negotiate with the family to get the bride.

Abram thinks, *If you're my wife, they'll kill me, and they'll marry you. You just tell them you're my sister. It's really not all that big a lie! In fact, it's partly true. Since you're my sister, if they want to marry you, they will negotiate with me. You know what I'll do, I'll set the price so high in the negotiation that nobody will be able to marry you. So we'll go down into Egypt, you act like my sister, I'll do the negotiations. Don't worry. I'm not going to let you go. No one will meet my demands.* This is not all in the text, but it seems to match Abram's logic and understanding of ancient cultures. It's a smooth plan—with one major oversight! There is only one person in all of Egypt exempted from the law of negotiation. Guess who it is? Big Pharaoh! He is the only person in all the land who is allowed to take a wife without negotiating.

When I Thought It Could Not Get Worse, It Did

"When Abram came to Egypt, the Egyptians saw that she was a very beautiful woman. And when Pharaoh's officials saw her, they praised her to Pharaoh, and she was taken into his palace" (Genesis 12:14, 15). Abram is in a mess! His airtight plan has busted. He has lost his wife. He is living a lie. He has no good options. In fact, he has only two options. First, he could go to Pharaoh and tell the truth—"Sarai is my wife." That's the truth. What are the consequences? Pharaoh will kill Abram and marry Sarai. What a wonderful option! In the second option, he can continue living the lie. Abram will live. Sarai will live, but Abram and Sarai will never be reunited.

I would say that Abram is in a mess. Can you see him sitting there in his tent?

Why did I come down to Egypt anyway?
Whose stupid idea was it to lie?
Why didn't Sarai stop me from lying?
She should never have allowed me to talk her into it.

While he is thinking all this through, here come a bunch of Pharaoh's servants. "O humble Abram, Pharaoh is so delighted in the beauty of Sarai that he is going to give you some cattle." In come the cattle.

What am I going to do?
I can't tell the truth, they'll kill me.
I have to keep on lying, but I can't.

While he struggles, Pharaoh sends more animals and servants. Abram is getting rich! He is the friend of Pharaoh! "He treated Abram well for her sake, and Abram acquired sheep and cattle, male and female donkeys, menservants and maidservants, and camels" (Genesis 12:16). The material possessions come in waves. Each reinforces Abram's dilemma, and the hole is dug deeper. You know what the bottom line is? There is no way out.

But you know the good news? God specializes in situations where there is no human escape. When you have dug the hole of your life so deep you cannot climb out, when you are overwhelmed with what's happening, when you declare, "There is no way out," you are precisely in a position for supernatural intervention.

Read carefully the record of God's intervention.

But the LORD inflicted serious diseases on Pharaoh and his household because of Abram's wife Sarai. So Pharaoh summoned Abram. "What have you done to me?" he said. "Why didn't you tell me she was your wife? Why did you say, 'She is my sister,' so that I took her to be my wife? Now then, here is your wife. Take her and go!" Then Pharaoh gave orders about Abram to his men, and they sent him on his way, with his wife and everything he had.

Genesis 12:17–20

What Do I Learn?

In pondering the failure of Abram, we have important lessons to learn.

We Are Tested Every Day

As believers we are challenged every day to trust God, obey God, and fear God.

Will I trust God, whatever my circumstances?
Will I obey God, whatever the consequences?
Will I fear God, whoever opposes me?

There Are Consequences When We Fail the Test

When we fail to trust, obey, or fear God, there are serious consequences. Abram did not experience the total impact of these until many years later. Read the following passage carefully.

Now Sarai, Abram's wife, had borne him no children. But she had an Egyptian maidservant named Hagar; so she said to Abram, "The LORD has kept me from having children. Go, sleep with my maidservant; perhaps I can build a family through her."

Genesis 16:1, 2

Abram attempts to build a family through Hagar—one of the maids he was given in Egypt. This was not God's plan. Hagar becomes the mother of the Arab nations. Sarai becomes the mother of the Jewish nation. Today, we live in the international tension between these countries, and the origin of the struggle goes back to Egypt. Abram failed to trust God. Abram failed to obey God. Abram failed to fear God. Today we feel the consequences of that terrible decision.

There Is Life Beyond Egypt (the Mess)

So Abram went up from Egypt to the Negev, with his wife and everything he had, and Lot went with him. Abram had become very wealthy in livestock and in silver and gold. From the Negev he went from place to place until he came to Bethel, to the place between Bethel and Ai where his tent had been earlier and where he had first built an altar. There Abram called on the name of the LORD.

Genesis 13:1–4

He goes back to Canaan. He goes back to *Bethel,* "the house of God." He goes back to the altar. Hallelujah—there is life beyond the mess.

Are you in Egypt?
Have you failed to trust God?
Have you failed to obey God?
Good news. There is life beyond the mess.

Prayer

Father, forgive me. I created my own mess. I thought I could do it on my own. I'm in Egypt. Please deliver me and bring me back. I've hurt myself and others. Heal the wounds. Thanks.

Chapter Three

All of Life
Is Making Right Decisions

Thirteen chapters in the Book of Genesis are devoted to the life and times of Abram; of these, five tell the story of Lot, his nephew.

Unlike Abram's story, Lot's describes complete failure. Why is so much space devoted to telling us about Lot's tragedy? His life offers a sharp contrast to Abram's. Lot represents the walk of sight, while Abram represents the walk of faith. Lot looks for a city built by human hands; Abram looks for a city whose builder is God. Lot fails; Abram succeeds. In both lives we see critical lessons that relate to our struggles today.

It Takes Two to Fight

So Abram went up from Egypt to the Negev, with his wife and everything he had, and Lot went with him. Abram had become very wealthy in livestock and in silver and gold. From the Negev he went from place to place until he came to Bethel, to the place between Bethel and Ai where his tent had been earlier.

Genesis 13:1–3

In a time of famine, Abram had gone down into Egypt to get food. In so doing he had turned his back on God and made a mess of his life. Note—he returns to where "his tent had been earlier."

Egypt represents the world, walking in the flesh. It always leads to disaster. But Abram returns to the altar of communion at Bethel.

Whenever we journey down into Egypt, we are doomed to failure. Whenever we fail to trust God or take our lives into our own hands to try to resolve our problems without the blessing and direction of God, we will always doom ourselves to failure. How do we get back on track? We have to do as Abram did and come back to the place where we messed up—Bethel, the house of God. Abram returns to an altar, which represents communion with God. At that significant location, Abram finally calls upon the Lord. Our path back to blessing begins at the altar and involves communion with God.

You know what I've discovered? Whenever I mess up, I begin by leaving the altar of communication with God; whenever I stop praying, I stop communing. I leave the altar in my life, and end up in Egypt, defeated and frustrated. So I have to make the long pilgrimage back to that altar of communion with God.

> Now Lot, who was moving about with Abram, also had flocks and herds and tents. But the land could not support them while they stayed together, for their possessions were so great that they were not able to stay together. And quarreling arose between Abram's herdsmen and the herdsmen of Lot. The Canaanites and Perizzites were also living in the land at that time.
>
> Genesis 13:5–7

The Canaanites and the Perizzites controlled the best grazing land. Abram and Lot entered this land with their flocks and herds. They soon discovered there was not enough pasture to accommodate both of their herds. So Abram offered a solution:

> So Abram said to Lot, "Let's not have any quarreling between you and me, or between your herdsmen and mine, for we are

brothers. Is not the whole land before you? Let's part company. If
you go to the left, I'll go to the right; if you go to the right, I'll
go to the left."

Genesis 13:8, 9

Abram refused to argue. Now you cannot have a fight if one
person refuses to be party to it. It takes two to make a quarrel, to
have a fight. There is nothing more frustrating than wanting a
good fight, only to discover that the other person is unwilling to
fight.

Abram decided, "I'm not going to fight. We're not going to
argue over this. We're not going to get mad at each other because
of the limited grazing land. I have a solution. The whole land is
before us. Lot, if you go to the right, I'll go to the left. If you go to
the left, I will go to the right. Let's part ways, but let's not have a
fight."

> Lot looked up and saw that the whole plain of the Jordan was
> well watered, like the garden of the LORD, like the land of Egypt,
> toward Zoar. (This was before the LORD destroyed Sodom and
> Gomorrah.) So Lot chose for himself the whole plain of the Jordan
> and set out toward the east. The two men parted company.
>
> Genesis 13:10, 11

Now Lot is about to make an important decision, one that
opens the door to a downward spiral of sin and destruction. He
looks at a patch of land, and it reminds him of Egypt. How did
Lot know it looked like Egypt? The obvious answer—he had seen
Egypt. When did he see Egypt? Abram took him there.

I hear people say, "Now if I go down into Egypt, the only person I affect is me. When I sin, I live with the consequences: I
don't affect others." Wrong! Lot comes to the crisis—*the most
significant* decision that he will ever make—and in that moment of

crisis he is influenced by an experience he had when Abram was disobedient to God. When I fail, it can have lasting consequences on the lives of others.

> The LORD said to Abram after Lot had parted from him, "Lift up your eyes from where you are and look north and south, east and west. All the land that you see I will give to you and your offspring forever. I will make your offspring like the dust of the earth, so that if anyone could count the dust, then your offspring could be counted. Go, walk through the length and breadth of the land, for I am giving it to you."
>
> Genesis 13:14–17

Think for just a moment what God is saying to Abram. He said, "Look around you. In every direction I am giving you the land. In fact, I am giving it to you and to your offspring forever." From Abram's point of view this was good news—but far from the reality he saw.

> *Reality 1:* The land was under the control of the Canaanites and Perizzites.
> *Reality 2:* The leftover grazing land belonged to Lot.
> *Reality 3:* NK—no kid. Sarai, his wife, is beyond the age of bearing children.

And God says:

> Go, walk through the length and breadth of the land, for I am giving it to you.
> I will make your offspring like the dust of the earth.

If I had been Abram, I would have negotiated the promise.

I know you're giving me the whole land. Do you think you might inform the Canaanites and Perizzites? In fact, I'd be happy with a couple of acres.

Offspring like the dust of the earth. Lord, just one kid would do!

What did Abram do? In the face of unbelievable odds, he built an altar to the Lord. You know what he is saying by building that altar? "Lord, I don't know how it is going to happen. I don't know how you are going to do it. It sounds impossible. But if you said it, I'm going to build the altar and trust you for the impossible." A man of faith.

The Problem with Lot

"So Lot chose for himself the whole plain of the Jordan and set out toward the east. The two men parted company" (Genesis 13:11).

All of life is making the right decisions! Now the decision that faced Lot didn't seem all that important. Am I going to go to the right, or am I going to go to the left? Do I take my herds over here, or do I take my herds over there? There is nothing profound about that choice, until you read the whole story. This simple decision opened up the door to a life of heartache, catastrophe, and failure. The lesson of Lot is the lesson of making the right decisions.

Lot made at least three mistakes when he made his decision.

Lot Chose Himself Ahead of Others

So Abram said to Lot, "Let's not have any quarreling between you and me, or between your herdsmen and mine, for we are brothers. Is not the whole land before you? Let's part company. If you go to the left, I'll go to the right; if you go to the right, I'll go to the left."

Genesis 13:8, 9

Abram says, "It's your choice, Lot!" Now custom, respect, and tradition required the following response: "Abram, you're the one whom God called out of Ur of the Chaldeans. You're the one whom I have followed to this part of the country. You're the one whom I followed into Egypt and out of Egypt. You are my elder. You make the choice. If you go to the left, I'll go to the right. If you go to the right, I will go to the left." But not so with Lot. Lot's focus is Lot. In the moment of pressure and decision, he decides for self-gratification. What he wanted—with little and perhaps no regard for what Abram and others thought.

Do you know what it means to walk by sight? It's getting ahead of yourself. It's stumbling over yourself. It's focusing the decisions of life in the context of me. Lot chose self over others— that was his first mistake.

Lot Chose His Occupation Over His Family

"Lot looked up and saw that the whole plain of the Jordan was well watered, like the garden of the LORD, like the land of Egypt, toward Zoar. (This was before the LORD destroyed Sodom and Gomorrah)" (Genesis 13:10). The well-watered plain of the Jordan was a good place to raise cattle. It was a horrible place to rear a family. Lot's decision was a sound business decision.

He chose the best grazing land.
He was near cities (Sodom and Gomorrah) where he could sell his products.

As a self-employed herdsman, Lot made a decision that would make a Harvard MBA proud. His only mistake was that he did not consider what the decision would do to his family. It destroyed his family (Genesis 19), and he lost them.

So Lot went out and spoke to his sons-in-law, who were pledged to marry his daughters. He said, "Hurry and get out of this place, because the LORD is about to destroy the city!" But his sons-in-law thought he was joking. With the coming of dawn, the angels urged Lot, saying, "Hurry! Take your wife and your two daughters who are here, or you will be swept away when the city is punished."

Genesis 19:14, 15

Imagine the tragedy of being mocked by your future sons-in-law, the tragedy of losing your own wife: "But Lot's wife looked back, and she became a pillar of salt" (Genesis 19:26).

Recently, I talked to someone in our church who refused promotions because they would necessitate his being away from his family and children on key holidays, like Christmas. He stayed at the same level to gain seniority so he could take off important days for his kids. After the kids were grown, he took the promotion.

When is the last time you made a decision related to a promotion with your family in mind?

Lot Chose the Immediate Over the Future.

Lot made the third mistake when he chose the immediate over the long term. He decided for something that made instant sense but ultimately destroyed his life. That's what Adam and Eve did, too. For a moment of personal gratification, they lost the long-term benefit of a relationship with God and plunged the human race into sin.

We live in a society that wants instant gratification. When we face choices, we need to ask ourselves: *What are the consequences beyond today? What are the consequences for next week? Next month? Next year? Ten years from now? What are the significant consequences of this decision?*

One of my fears as a pastor is that I'll make some decisions now without the spiritual foresight of the long-term consequences. I pray constantly, "Dear God, help me to see the larger picture. Help me to see the long range. Help me not to make any decision in my personal life that looks good right now, but is ultimately destined for destruction." That's why I lean so heavily on the godly advice and supervision of the leadership of Calvary Church.

Mack

We've seen that Lot made three critical mistakes:

1. He chose self over others.
2. He chose his occupation over his family.
3. He chose the immediate over the future.

Given that all of life is making the right decisions, how do I go about doing it? Think of the word *Mack*. Run your decisions up against a Mack truck.

1. M—Motive: What Is My Motive? What is my motive in this decision—self or others? Am I making this decision purely motivated by what it will do for me, or am I considering its impact on others?

2. A—Affect: How Will It Affect My Convictions? Later in the life of Lot, we will discover that cooperation with the world leads to contamination and ultimately compromise with it. There is a spiral that leads us farther and farther down, until we violate our own values. Ask yourself, *How will this affect my beliefs and values?*

"We want you to become a full partner in the firm, but you know we do things a little bit differently from the way religious people do them. We're not going to ask you to do anything really bad, but you've got to understand that in the world in which we live, you know, there are a few corners that you have to cut."

Better not to have a job than to have one that necessitates the lowering of your Christian values and convictions. Because once you open the door to the world, before long you are contaminated and are doing the very things that contradict your commitment to Jesus Christ. How will this affect my belief system? I would rather stand before God dirt poor, without compromising, than offer God my portfolio and all of my accomplishments, having cut corners and compromised my convictions. God, keep us true to your word and to what it means to be a Christian.

3. C—Consequences: What Are the Long-term Consequences? What will result from this decision? As I look beyond the decision, what are the ultimate consequences? Lot couldn't see it! All he saw was a bunch of grass on a plain. Yet the text tells us that Sodom and Gomorrah were there.

4. K—Kids: How Will It Affect My Kid(s)? Have you thought about that? Much of the corporate world is no friend to the family, though it's beginning to change a little. However, often a successful business person spends a year here, two years there, two years somewhere else. You ask the kids, "Where did you go to school?" and they have no idea how to begin answering the question. "I went to school everywhere!" they have to explain.

What about the kids? When Lorna and I were thinking of coming to Grand Rapids, our biggest concern was our children. How would a move affect them? One of our kids really struggled for over a year. He would cry and sob at night, because he wanted to go back to Lynchburg.

I got to the point of saying, "Well, God, you worked so supernaturally in bringing us here. You're working in the church. It means nothing, God, if my kids aren't happy." I know you can say, "God brought you here, make them happy!" That's my style, but that doesn't work. I even got to the point of saying, "Well,

God, if you can't work this out, maybe I ought to go back to Lynchburg." I really struggled in my heart. Eventually God brought happiness and satisfaction, but it took more than a year.

Who cares whether my congregation has over 4,000 in attendance on Sunday morning, if the needs of my wife and my kids are not being met? I've got too many friends who pastor churches bigger than mine who have no time for their families. I struggle daily to make the decisions that put my family ahead of what I am called to do in my church.

I grew up seeing pastors work harder than anybody, get up earlier than anybody, go to bed later than anybody, put in more hours than anybody, and make more phone calls than anybody. I grew up with the understanding that a pastor needs his car parked out in front of the church before anyone goes to work, so when they pass by they can look in the parking lot and see his car there. When they go home at night, his car is still there, and whenever someone calls, he's waiting for that call.

Sometimes Lorna tries not to let me answer the phone at home. I'd like to have three or four lines and be talking to six people all at the same time. That's my idea of a good time—working. But all of that means nothing if I don't spend time with my family. It's the *K*, and it's the kicker! *How will this decision affect my children, my family?*

Footnote on the Family

Preaching is tough—especially when you have to practice what you preach. The week after I waxed eloquent on putting your kids ahead of your job, I was forced to decide whether I was willing to do it. The next Tuesday was the monthly board meeting. That was also the night of my eight-year-old daughter Heather's public school program. What was I going to do? Part of me said, "You need to be at that board meeting. That is your monthly obligation. It's the first Tuesday after the first Wednesday of every month. It's been that way since 1929, and you are obligated to be there." The other part of me objected, "Heather couldn't care less what the board does. She doesn't even know what the board is. To her the most significant event of Tuesday night is the program at the elementary school." I decided that if I was going to preach it, I'd better live it. So I talked to Dick Doyle, the vice-chairman. I explained, "Dick, I'm not going to be at the first part of the board meeting. I'm going to be out in Rockford, watching Heather in her school program. I'll get there as quickly as I can, but I'm going to stay for the whole program." And I did.

I rushed all the way back to the church, and the board had already dismissed! It made me realize the significant contribution that I have made to the ministry of this church. One hour and fifteen minutes, and they were out of there! Gone! It normally took three hours when I attended.

Dancing with the Devil Will Wear You Out

During my doctoral studies at the University of Virginia, I took a course entitled, "The Statewide Coordination of Higher Education." We spent time discussing the virtue of federal and state funding for universities and colleges and studied all the government regulations that accompanied funding. I shall never forget the example used by the professor to illustrate the relationship between the government and colleges. He said that receiving money from the government was like dancing. "The government invites you to dance," he told us. "And when you get on the floor, you discover you're dancing with an octopus!"

Dancing with the devil is the same way. The initial invitation looks good, but you soon discover you are entangled in sin and cannot escape. Lot's life illustrates how sin ultimately strangles your spiritual life. In the tragic unfolding of his life we discover several important principles about how sin entangles us.

Sin Is Often One Small Step at a Time in the Wrong Direction

Lot did not mess up his life all at once. Rather, it was the cumulative effect of a series of small steps.

Step 1: He looked. "Lot looked up and saw that the whole plain of the Jordan was well watered, like the garden of the LORD, like the land of Egypt, toward Zoar. (This was before the LORD destroyed Sodom and Gomorrah.)" (Genesis 13:10). It starts so simply. There is nothing profound about that statement. But that first step led Lot to a point of compromise with the world. He looked, and he saw. What starts as a simple look can lead to devastating consequences.

Consider Eve. The Scriptures state that when she "*saw* that the fruit of the tree was good for food and pleasing to the eye . . . she took some and ate it" (Genesis 3:6, *italics added*).

Consider David. "One evening David got up from his bed and walked around on the roof of the palace. From the roof he *saw* a woman bathing" (2 Samuel 11:2, *italics added*). David committed adultery with her, had her husband murdered, and married her as if nothing had happened. Jesus warns us that "anyone who *looks* at a woman lustfully has already committed adultery with her in his heart" (Matthew 5:28, *italics added*).

When Satan tempted Christ, he *showed* him all the kingdoms of the world.

We are warned to avoid the world.

> Do not love the world or anything in the world. If anyone loves the world, the love of the Father is not in him. For everything in the world—the craving of sinful man, the lust of his eyes and the boasting of what he has and does—comes not from the Father but

from the world. The world and its desires pass away, but the man
who does the will of God lives forever.

1 John 2:15–17

Step 2: He pitched his tent near Sodom. "Abram lived in the
land of Canaan, while Lot lived among the cities of the plain and
pitched his tents near Sodom" (Genesis 13:12).

Lot knew that the cities of Sodom and Gomorrah were exceed-
ingly sinful. That was not the place to be. To Lot's credit, he didn't
move into Sodom. He pitched his tents near the cities. Perhaps
he felt that locating near these urban centers provided him with a
business advantage. However, he ignored the ever-present danger of getting too close to sin and temptation. Sin may affect us or
the people around us. In Lot's case, it was the people around
him—his family.

Step 3: He moved into Sodom. "The two angels arrived at
Sodom in the evening, and Lot was sitting in the gateway of the
city. When he saw them, he got up to meet them and bowed down
with his face to the ground" (Genesis 19:1).

Many years have passed since Lot and Abram parted ways.
Lot is now living in Sodom. In fact, he is sitting at the gate. Now
that's an important statement. In ancient culture, when you arrived
at the gates of the walled city, the civil, religious, and political
leaders would be sitting there. The leadership sitting at the gate
transacted all the business of the city.

Note the steps that Lot took. He looked. He moved near
Sodom. He became a leader of Sodom. Tragically, in the New
Testament we read that every single day Lot's soul was vexed
because of the sin of that city. While he transacted the business,
while he sat with the leadership, while he participated in the city,
his conscience struggled with the sin.

And if he rescued Lot, a righteous man, who was distressed by
the filthy lives of lawless men (for that righteous man, living
among them day after day, was tormented in his righteous soul
by the lawless deeds he saw and heard.

2 Peter 2:7, 8

The downward spiral of sin is often a series of small steps.
You usually do not run out and commit gross sin. I am sure, had
we been able to interview Lot, when he stood making his decision, and had we described for him the ultimate consequence of
his life, he would have laughed. "No way would I ever compromise with the world. After all, I know God's righteousness. No
way would my family be destroyed like that. No way would I
participate in the politics of Sodom. Impossible! It cannot happen to me." Sin always begins with simple decisions.

Whenever I am talking with people who have gone through a
time when they absolutely went contrary to the Word of God, I
find they did not intend to do it. They did not plan to get involved
in sin. It began with simple decisions—not reading the Bible on a
daily basis, not spending time in prayer, starting to skip church
and avoiding accountability with other believers. What didn't
seem like all that big a deal began to build until that person found
himself vulnerable to sin and ended up doing the very things that
he thought he would never do. Sin always begins with the look,
the simple decisions of everyday life.

Sin Is Unreasonable in Its Effect

Sin makes us do stupid things. It powerfully dominates our
lives and causes us to do unreasonable and illogical things. You
know what I have learned? Don't ever ask anyone who has sinned
why he did it, because he doesn't have a good answer. It's just
like asking your kids why they did what they did. Has your son
ever had a logical, reasonable answer for what he did? Ninety

percent of the time—no! I learned this when I was in the university, in student affairs. I was the final appeal on all dismissals. I learned not to ask students why they did what they did. Most of the time they said, "I don't know." That's how sin is. It causes us to do those things that seem unreasonable.

This is evident in the life of Lot, as recorded in Genesis 19. Two angels have arrived in Sodom to warn Lot that God is going to destroy the city. The men of Sodom, who practice homosexuality, gather around the door where Lot lives and demand that Lot send the two male angels out, so they can have an orgy all night long. Lot refuses their request and offers them an unbelievable alternative:

> Look, I have two daughters who have never slept with a man. Let me bring them out to you, and you can do what you like with them. But don't do anything to these men, for they have come under the protection of my roof.
>
> Genesis 19:8

I have a daughter, and I love her very much. I cannot even stretch my mind to understand why Lot, who loved his daughters, would offer them to a sex-crazed crowd for a mass orgy. How could any father stoop to such depths? This reckless act defies human nature, the bonds of marriage, the instincts of a father, and everything that is natural. It defies family relationships. Yet he did it! Why? The only explanation is that sin does not make sense! When our value systems are distorted, when we have compromised what we believe, when we are dominated by a wicked environment, and when we are silent about what we believe, we will do and say things that defy our faith.

Why do so many pastors mess up? It defies everything they preach, everything they've taught, their relationship with God, and their relationship with their families. Why would someone go out and defy everything that he believes? Because sin does not make sense. It can cause us to do the very things that we despise. That's why we ought to make no compromise with sin. We must avoid even the appearance of evil. We must live lives that are separated from the world and separated unto the Lord. Sin is insidious in its beginning and unreasonable in its effect.

Sin Is Destructive in Its Power

By the time Lot reached Zoar, the sun had risen over the land. Then the LORD rained down burning sulfur on Sodom and Gomorrah—from the LORD out of the heavens. Thus he overthrew those cities and the entire plain, including all those living in the cities— and also the vegetation in the land. But Lot's wife looked back, and she became a pillar of salt.

Genesis 19:23–26

God judged Sodom and Lot's family. An entire civilization was wiped out. Lot lost his entire family, with the exception of two daughters. Lot lost his business and property.

When we disobey God, we cannot escape the consequences of our sin:

Do not be deceived: God cannot be mocked. A man reaps what he sows. The one who sows to please his sinful nature, from that nature will reap destruction; the one who sows to please the Spirit, from the Spirit will reap eternal life.

Galatians 6:7, 8

But there is good news:

He who conceals his sins does not prosper, but whoever confesses and renounces them finds mercy.

Proverbs 28:13

If we confess our sins, he is faithful and just and will forgive us our sins and purify us from all unrighteousness. If we claim we have not sinned, we make him out to be a liar and his word has no place in our lives.

1 John 1:9, 10

We all mess up. Thank you, Lord, for your mercy and forgiveness. God is the God of the second chance. The above verses need little explanation. They offer hope, forgiveness, and a new beginning to those who find themselves dancing with the devil. God can break the power and penalty of sin through Jesus Christ.

Prayer

Lord, it's easy to look back and see the bad decisions I made. It's incredibly difficult to look ahead to the potential consequences of each decision. Since you know the future, give me wisdom to make decisions that will please you and benefit my family. Thanks.

Chapter Four

Going After People Is a Pain in the Neck

Ministry is Christ-centered and people-related. Both ingredients are necessary to carry out the mission of the church. The problem is that once you get involved with people it gets messy. People hurt each other; they let you down. Once you get serious about helping people, you have entered an uncontrollable variable into ministry. Frankly, working with people can be a pain in the neck.

Abram discovered the cost in time, effort, and resources that resulted from getting involved with people.

I Have Had Enough

At this time Amraphel king of Shinar, Arioch king of Ellasar, Kedorlaomer king of Elam and Tidal king of Goiim went to war against Bera king of Sodom, Birsha king of Gomorrah, Shinab king of Admah, Shemeber king of Zeboiim, and the king of Bela (that is, Zoar). All these latter kings joined forces in the Valley of Siddim (the Salt Sea). For twelve years they had been subject to Kedorlaomer, but in the thirteenth year they rebelled.

Genesis 14:1–4

Verse 1 mentions four kings from Asia, several hundred miles east of Palestine. The five kings mentioned in verse 2 are kings of city-states located in the Jordan Valley; Sodom and Gomorrah were two of those cities.

Now these five kings and their walled cities in the Jordan Valley were all under submission to Kedorlaomer ("Big K") and the three kings that allied with him. The city-state kings paid taxes to the four kings in Asia for twelve years. And then, *they had had enough!* In the thirteenth year, they rebelled.

> In the fourteenth year, Kedorlaomer and the kings allied with him went out and defeated the Rephaites in Ashteroth Karnaim, the Zuzites in Ham, the Emites in Shaveh Kiriathaim and the Horites in the hill country of Seir, as far as El Paran near the desert.
>
> Genesis 14:5, 6

Remember, news did not travel fast. It took a year for "Big K" to get the word and to form an alliance to punish these rebellious kings. In verses 5 through 7, Kedorlaomer and three other kings begin a long march from Iran, through modern-day Iraq, all the way over to Damascus and modern-day Syria. They journeyed directly south along the east side of the Jordan River, until they arrived at the desert, south of the Dead Sea. Then they turned north into the valley, where they engaged in war with the five city-states. Along the way they had some preliminary bouts (called wars) to warm them up for the title fight with the five city-states. They fought the Rephaites (v. 5). This word means "long stretched." They were probably a fierce tribe of giant warriors. Next they fought the Zuzites (v. 5). The Zuzites were probably related to the Rephaites and were a tall and fierce people. Next, they fought the Emites (v. 5). The word *Emite* means "fierce and terrible." Then they fought the Horites, who were cave dwellers. This demanded a different battle strategy from the one used with the Rephaites, the Zuzites, and the Emites. Finally, they fought the Amalekites and the Amorites (v. 7).

Now four kings from Asia have marched with fury and strength to punish the five kings in the Jordan Valley. Along the way they have defeated two tribes of giants and a group known as the "fierce and terrible." They have adjusted their battle strategy and defeated the cave dwellers. Then they have moved south of the city-states and have conquered all the territory. No one has been able to stand in their way. They are now ready to do battle with the five-king alliance.

> Then the king of Sodom, the king of Gomorrah, the king of Admah, the king of Zeboiim and the king of Bela (that is, Zoar) marched out and drew up their battle lines in the Valley of Siddim against Kedorlaomer king of Elam, Tidal king of Goiim, Amraphel king of Shinar and Arioch king of Ellasar—four kings against five.
>
> Genesis 14:8, 9

Apparently it was not much of a battle. The kings of Sodom and Gomorrah fled! Some of their men fell into tar pits (tar was used for mortar in ancient buildings).

The first eleven verses of this chapter serve as the introduction to the problem of verse 12 (the problem of Lot): "They also carried off Abram's nephew Lot and his possessions, since he was living in Sodom" (Genesis 14:12).

Abram Went in Pursuit

> One who had escaped came and reported this to Abram the Hebrew. Now Abram was living near the great trees of Mamre the Amorite, a brother of Eshcol and Aner, all of whom were allied with Abram. When Abram heard that his relative had been taken

captive, he called out the 318 trained men born in his household
and went in pursuit as far as Dan.

Genesis 14:13, 14

Abram's immediate response to this crisis was to go "in pursuit." He had not made a casual decision. The first phase of the
campaign involved a journey from Mamre to Dan (140 miles
north). The second phase of the campaign extended farther north
to Hobah, near Damascus (v. 15). This involved traveling another
100 miles.

Abram and his army went over 240 miles, one way, to rescue
Lot. *Why?* Part of the answer is in the language used to describe
Lot. "When Abram heard that *his relative* had been taken captive" (v. 14, *italics added*). The word translated "relative" could
also be translated "brother." One of the compelling arguments for
pursuit was the fact that Lot was Abram's brother. Lot had made
many bad decisions. He lived in a wicked city. He was more interested in his business than his family. He had clearly made poor
choices and maybe even deserved to live with the consequences of
these choices—but Abram pursued anyway. After all, Lot was
his "brother." "A friend loves at all times, and a brother is born for
adversity" (Proverbs 17:17).

It's Not My Problem

We live in a culture that hesitates getting involved with others. We often don't even know our neighbors. We complain about
the problems of AIDS, pornography, drugs, alcohol, and so on,
but we seldom get involved to make a difference. In our society
we can observe muggings and robberies without dialing 911—
we don't want to get involved.

The same is true in the church. We walk away from our own
wounded. We ignore those who fail. We let brothers and sisters

struggle alone in the darkness. And we justify our paralysis with verses from the Bible.

Abram had a couple of options in regard to Lot. He didn't have to get involved either.

1. The Theological Option. The theological option is to accept that Lot is getting what he deserves. After all, he made a bad decision. He moved into a wicked city. He lowered his standards. He compromised with the world. Now that the city has been conquered and Lot taken captive, he is getting what he deserves. If he had *not* been living in Sodom, he would *not* have been taken captive.

I hear Christians talk like that today. Recently we got involved as a church with the issue of AIDS in the Grand Rapids community. I visited with the people who oversee the AIDS Resource Center in Grand Rapids; it is the central coordinating structure for all that relates to AIDS in our community. I also spent an afternoon with the pastor of the Metropolitan Community Church in our city (this church accepts monogamous homosexuality as a biblical expression of sexuality). He is the most knowledgeable person in our community on the subject of AIDS (and a very compassionate and caring person). To make a long story short—our church became involved in helping people with AIDS.

What has surprised me is the reaction of some Christians to our involvement. They see AIDS as a homosexual issue (which it is *not*). Their attitude is "If homosexuals would stop doing what they are doing, they would stop getting what they are getting. Moreover, they deserve what they get. Leave them alone."

The same attitude is prevalent in regard to Christians who "mess up" (and who hasn't "messed up"!). Consider the person who used to come to church, read the Scriptures, and pray and grow. Then she made some bad choices. She made some decisions contrary to the Word of God, and she found her life all messed up somewhere around Damascus, far from home. What is our response?

"Well, she's getting what she deserves! You know she made a bad decision! Now she has to live with the consequences."

Now I am not saying that there are not consequences for bad decisions—there are. But the point of this story is that Abram understood all of this, yet without hesitation went in pursuit.

2. The Sovereignty Option. The second option open to Abram was to leave Lot's deliverance up to God. After all, Lot got himself in this mess. Since God is in control, he allowed it to happen. Therefore, God can take care of Lot. Now that also sounds very religious and extremely spiritual and ultrapious. Yes, Lot made some bad choices. Yes, he has been taken captive. Yes, he is far from the Lord and far from home. But let God worry about it. Not Abram! Abram understood the sovereignty of God. He understood the power of God. He understood the direction of God. The text *still* says that Abram went *in pursuit* of *his brother*. This principle is clearly stated in the New Testament: "Therefore, as we have opportunity, let us do good to all people, especially to those who belong to the family of believers" (Galatians 6:10).

Going After People
Takes a Great Personal Sacrifice

When you make the choice to help someone, it will inevitably demand personal sacrifice. If you do not want to make sacrifices, don't get involved with people. The cost to Abram was exceptional.

1. He Made a Choice Against All Odds. Abram gathered an army of 318 (v. 14) and went in pursuit of an eastern army that had not lost a battle. That army had defeated the giants, the fierce and terrible, the cave dwellers, the Amorites, and five different cities. Although we do not know how large their army was, it was certainly bigger than 318 men. But Abram defied the overwhelming odds and moved in pursuit.

Sometimes, in our relationships with fallen and hurting people, we count the odds. "Well what are the odds of her coming back to the Lord?" "How reasonable is it to believe that if I pursue him I will be successful?" "If it's not genuine, in a few months she'll be back where she was." The issue is not being successful! The issue is pursuing. Abram made his choice in spite of the odds.

2. He Made a Choice That Demanded All His Resources. The choice to pursue involved Abram's entire army (v. 14). It cost all of his resources. If we are to be involved with hurting people, it will cost everything we have.

Did you know that it is highly inconvenient to work with people? At times, it is a pain in the neck. It costs to be involved with hurting, struggling, captive people. Though it cost Abram all of his resources, he willingly risked everything he had to go in pursuit of a brother who never should have been in the city of Sodom in the first place.

3. He Made a Choice That Demanded His Personal Involvement. "During the night Abram divided his men to attack them and he routed them, pursuing them as far as Hobah, north of Damascus. He recovered all the goods and brought back his relative Lot and his possessions, together with the women and the other people" (Genesis 14:15, 16).

If I had been Abram I would have been the administrator. I would have mapped out the strategy and said, "Fellows, they went that way! When you defeat them, I'll be here to meet you." I would have stayed at home with the joint chiefs of staff and handled the daily press briefings.

Abram got involved! He understood the odds. He committed his resources and said, "I will do something about it. I will get involved, even if it means traveling to Damascus and 100 miles north of Damascus. If it requires 240 miles, I'll do it. I will pursue my brother till I find him." In verse 14 we read that he called the trained men in his house "to turn out." That verb literally means "to pour out." What better way to describe our pursuit of hurting people than literally taking our lives and pouring them out for the pursuit and restoration of others.

4. He Made the Choice to Spend Time. When you really get involved in pursuing people, it takes significant amounts of time. It would have been easier to order Lot, "If you're up in Damascus, start by getting right with God. Figure a way to sneak off from 'Big K.' Then come on back home." But when you get involved with struggling, hurting people who, because of choices that they have made, find themselves captive and far from home, it requires *time*! Abram was willing to give of himself, to give of his resources, to give of his time, to face unbelievable odds, to do everything that was necessary to pursue and to rescue his brother Lot.

If you are too busy with life, don't pursue fallen people. You will only disappoint them and hurt yourself, because pursuing those people will demand significant amounts of time. Don't pursue too many people. It can leave you exhausted and of little use to yourself, others, or God.

5. He Made a Choice Without Regard to the Consequences. Was Abram successful? Yes and no.

Yes, he was successful. He rescued Lot: "He recovered all the goods and brought back his relative Lot and his possessions, together with the women and the other people" (Genesis 14:16).

No, he was *not* successful: He delivered Lot from the eastern kings, but Lot went right back to Sodom, where he eventually messed up his life and family.

Now if I had been Lot, I would at least have asked God what he was trying to teach me! I was living in a city of sin. I was carried off, captive, with everything that I possessed. Abram came after me and rescued me. I would at least ask, "What are you trying to teach me, God?" You don't have to be superintelligent to figure out that maybe God was telling Lot that he ought not to be living in the wicked city of Sodom.

Did Lot learn the lesson? No! No! No! After all the effort and all the time and all the commitment and all the resources, Lot went right back to Sodom. In a few chapters we'll discover how his entire life was shattered.

Now from a human point of view, Abram wasted his time and resources. He went to a lot of trouble and headache and inconvenience to rescue Lot. Lot should not have been in Sodom in the first place, but he returned there. Abram pursued Lot with no guarantee of success and no preconditions for Lot's response. The principle is this: You do what is right. You put the Scriptures into practice. You leave the consequences up to God. "Brothers, if someone is caught in a sin, you who are spiritual should restore him gently. But watch yourself, or you also may be tempted" (Galatians 6:1).

Pursuing People Is an Act of Faith and Love

Why did Abram pursue Lot? It was a choice that exacted a toll on his resources. He pursued Lot:

1. Against all odds
2. Committing all his resources
3. Demanding his personal involvement
4. Consuming his time
5. With no guarantee of results

Why? Because he was a man of faith.

Faith is not simply an intellectual affirmation to the truth of God's Word; it transforms our life. Faith that does not produce in us love and compassion for others is *not* true faith. Show me a Christian who is always critical of others who make mistakes, who self-righteously puts down brothers and sisters who get led captive up to Damascus, who has little warmth and love and forgiveness for those who make mistakes, who is unwilling to pursue those who are hurting, and I will show you a Christian who is not behaving like a Christian. Faith that is not translated into works of love and compassion is not saving faith.

The answer to the question as to why Abram would go after Lot is simple! He was a person of faith.

> What good is it, my brothers, if a man claims to have faith but has no deeds? Can such faith save him? Suppose a brother or sister is without clothes and daily food. If one of you says to him, "Go, I wish you well; keep warm and well fed," but does nothing about his physical needs, what good is it? In the same way, faith by itself, if it is not accompanied by action, is dead.
>
> James 2:14–17

We Pursue Others Because God Pursued Us

The second reason we pursue others is that God pursued us. No biblical story illustrates that principle better than the story of Hosea and Gomer. God asked the prophet Hosea to marry a prostitute named Gomer. Chapters 1 and 2 of Hosea describe that marriage. They have three children—a boy, a girl, and a boy. After the third child, Hosea discovers that the children that he thought were his were somebody else's.

Throughout their marriage Gomer is unfaithful. She leaves him. It's a tragic story of Gomer's journey from one man to another man to another man to another man. All during this period of unfaithfulness, Hosea continues to love his wife. In fact, he secretly gives money, grain, and wine to her while she lives adulterously with others (2:8). Gomer accepts these gifts and offers them as sacrifices to Baal.

Gomer is finally sold into slavery. She is put on the open market by one of her husbands. Stripped naked, she stands in the marketplace and is sold to the highest bidder. If anyone deserves to be sold into slavery it's this wife who has been repeatedly unfaithful. In the crowd that day is Hosea. To the shock of the crowd, he enters the bidding contest. He offers the highest bid and buys back his unfaithful wife. He asks her to live with him. Notice the intent of his incredible love story.

> The LORD said to me, "Go, show your love to your wife again, though she is loved by another and is an adulteress. Love her as the LORD loves the Israelites, though they turn to other gods and love the sacred raisin cakes."
>
> Hosea 3:1

"Love her as the LORD loves the Israelites." Why do we pursue those who have fallen into sin? Why do we pour ourselves out whatever the cost, whatever the odds, whatever the time, whatever the consequences? Why do we spend our effort and our prayers and our energies going after people who have made bad decisions? Because we are to love them just as God loved us! God loved us when we were in rebellion against him! God loves us when *we* move into the city of Sodom. He loves us when *we* make bad choices. He loves us when *we* find ourselves captive. God still loves us!

> This is how God showed his love among us: He sent his one and only Son into the world that we might live through him. This is love: not that we loved God, but that he loved us and sent his Son as an atoning sacrifice for our sins.
>
> 1 John 4:9–10

We ought to be committed (whatever the cost, whatever the odds, whatever the sacrifice, whatever the time, whatever the consequences) to pursuing hurting, struggling people because God continues to pursue us in his love.

Once I understand the unconditional love of God for Ed Dobson, I will pursue others. God loves me in spite of my failures, in spite of my mistakes, in spite of my selfishness, in spite of my pride. I have experienced that love. I am to love, to pray, to pour out, to plead, beseech and pursue and pursue and pursue and pursue and pursue, until, like Gomer, they are drawn back to Christ by unconditional love.

Prayer

Father, some of us have children like Lot, who made bad decisions. They have lived in ways that displease you. They are miles away from home. I pray for their moms and dads. Help them not to give up, because You don't. Give them courage to keep praying and to keep crying and to keep loving and to keep reaching out.

I pray for those who have made some very bad decisions—sinful decisions. Help us to pursue them and pray for them. Help us to be people of faith, knowing that with you nothing is impossible. Lord, humble us. Remind us that we are to be gentle. May we never rejoice when a brother or sister falls into sin, but may we be broken. Help us never to be arrogant or self-righteous. Help us not to shoot your own wounded children. Remind us of Abram, who poured himself out for his brother, and it appears that his brother was ungrateful. Thank you, God, for not giving up on us. Thank you for pursuing us and pursuing us until we stood at the foot of the cross and laid the burden of our sin and guilt there.

For those who have been taken captive, help them to know that there is deliverance. Let them know your forgiveness and healing. May we do everything in such a way as to demonstrate our unconditional love for others. Lay upon our hearts those who are struggling, and may we love them back to you. In Jesus' name, I pray, Amen.

Chapter Five

God Has a People— and They Don't All Wear the Same Label

Grand Rapids, Michigan, is considered by many Christians a "mainstream" evangelical city. It is the home of many Christian publishers and Christian organizations and ministries. There are 480 Protestant churches in Grand Rapids. The largest church in the city is the Catholic Church. Every Saturday, an entire section of the newspaper is devoted to religious news and advertising. There are also several Christian colleges and seminaries in the city. The ghosts of John Calvin and other theologians loom over the skyline.

One of the religious phenomena of Grand Rapids is the fishbowl theory. Whenever a new pastor, church, or organization comes to the city, people leave the fishbowl where they were attending and get into the new fishbowl—until a newer fishbowl comes along. Consequently, a lot of church decline or growth is attributed to switching fishbowls. The vast unchurched community (over 60 percent) must look with wonder and amazement at this uniquely religious community.

With the number and variety of churches in this community, labels become important to each group. They identify and separate us from others:

Christian Reformed
Roman Catholic
Baptist
Nazarene
Assembly of God
Episcopal
Presbyterian
Methodist
Christian Missionary Alliance
Full Gospel

There are many congregations, but there is only one church—
the body of Christ. God has a people, and they don't all wear the
same label. This is the lesson that Abram is about to learn in his
interaction with Melchizedek.

God Is Our Ultimate Source

Abram defeated the kings from Asia and returned home with
the captured people and goods.

> He recovered all the goods and brought back his relative Lot
> and his possessions, together with the women and the other people.
> After Abram returned from defeating Kedorlaomer and the
> kings allied with him, the king of Sodom came out to meet him in
> the Valley of Shaveh (that is, the King's Valley).
>
> Genesis 14:16, 17

When Abram returned from defeating the Asian king, the king of
Sodom came out to meet him (v. 17). The deliverer (Abram) met
the delivered (king of Sodom). Abram brings back both the property that was taken and the people who had been captured. As a
token of gratitude, the king of Sodom suggested that Abram keep
the goods and property. Abram's response is most significant.

> But Abram said to the king of Sodom, "I have raised my hand to the LORD, God Most High, Creator of heaven and earth, and have taken an oath—that I will accept nothing belonging to you, not even a thread or the thong of a sandal, so that you will never be able to say, 'I made Abram rich.' I will accept nothing but what my men have eaten and the share that belongs to the men who went with me—to Aner, Eshcol and Mamre. Let them have their share."
>
> Genesis 14:22–24

Abram was certainly entitled to some type of payment. He had made great personal sacrifice in going to battle for Lot and the people of Sodom. But Abram declined the offer. He understood that *God was his ultimate source*. Abram had taken an oath ("raised my hand") before El Elyon (the Most High God) that he would accept nothing other than what his men deserved. He did not want anyone to conclude that the king of Sodom made him rich. He wanted others to know that his God had blessed him.

Our source of blessing is God. Our ultimate source is God. That's easy to state, but difficult to live. I tend to rely on my own ability as my source. I tend to turn to others for help when life is tough. But living the life of faith is trusting in God *alone* as our source. Carlo Carretto in the book *I, Francis* states this objective well:

> To bear witness, to testify, to myself and to other human beings, that God alone sufficed for me, and that I did not have to be concerned about anything, anything at all—think of the flowers of the field; they never have to spin or weave; yet not even Solomon in all his regalia was like one of these (Luke 12:27).

The Mystery of Melchizedek

> Then Melchizedek king of Salem brought out bread and wine. He was priest of God Most High, and he blessed Abram, saying, "Blessed be Abram by God Most High, Creator of heaven and earth. And blessed be God Most High, who delivered your enemies into your hand."
>
> Genesis 14:18–20

Notice the simple facts of this meeting between Abram and Melchizedek.

1. The name *Melchizedek* means "king of righteousness."
2. The name *Salem* means "peace." It may refer to the ancient site of Jeru*salem*.
3. Melchizedek brought bread and wine to Abram.
4. Melchizedek was a priest of El Elyon (the Most High God), whom Abram worshiped (v. 22).
5. Melchizedek blessed Abram.
6. Abram gave a tenth of his possessions to Melchizedek. This was a common practice during Abram's day. People often gave tithes to their gods as a form of worship and thanksgiving.

Who is Melchizedek? If this were the only time he was mentioned in the Bible, then the answer would be simple. Melchizedek is a king and priest who was a contemporary of Abram and to whom Abram presented tithes. However, two other passages of Scripture mention Melchizedek, and this fuels an ongoing debate as to who he was or is.

"The LORD has sworn and will not change his mind: 'You are a priest forever, in the order of Melchizedek'" (Psalm 110:4). This is what is called a messianic psalm—a psalm that prophesies the coming of Messiah. It emphasizes two dimensions of his coming. First, he is coming as king. Second, he is coming as a priest. Psalm 110:1–3 describes his mighty reign; verse 4 describes the coming of Messiah as priest, in fact, a very unique priest: "You are a priest forever, in the order of Melchizedek." An "order" is a grouping of priests. The Messiah will not be a priest after the order of Aaron—the regular Old Testament priest. Rather, he will come as a unique priest, after the order of Melchizedek.

So Melchizedek is an important individual because he is connected in some way to the coming of Messiah. This connection is further explored in the Bible's last reference to Melchizedek:

> This Melchizedek was king of Salem and priest of God Most High. He met Abraham returning from the defeat of the kings and blessed him, and Abraham gave him a tenth of everything. First, his name means "king of righteousness"; then also, "king of Salem" means "king of peace." Without father or mother, without genealogy, without beginning of days or end of life, like the Son of God he remains a priest forever.
>
> Hebrews 7:1–3

In this chapter of Hebrews, the writer demonstrates the superiority of Jesus Christ over all other Old Testament priests. The substance of his argument is as follows: Abram gave tithes to Melchizedek, therefore Melchizedek is greater than Abram. The Old Testament priests are descendants of Abram. Since Melchizedek is greater than Abram, he is greater than all of Abraham's descendants. The priesthood of Aaron is descended from Abram, therefore Melchizedek is greater than the Old Testament priests. Jesus is a priest after the order of Melchizedek. Melchizedek is greater than Abram and Abram's descendants (including the priesthood of Aaron), therefore Jesus is greater than Abram and the priesthood of Aaron.

This passage also describes more of the characteristics of Melchizedek. "Without father or mother, without genealogy, without beginning of days or end of life, like the Son of God he remains a priest forever" (Hebrews 7:3).

Melchizedek is:

1. King of righteousness
2. King of peace
3. Without father and mother
4. Without genealogy
5. Without beginning of days
6. Without end of life
7. Like the Son of God
8. A priest forever

Given all this information, who is Melchizedek? The critical issue we must deal with is the meaning of the above "without" statements. There are three possibilities.

1. Some believe Melchizedek was an angel. This would explain his lack of genealogy, parents, beginning and end of days.
2. Some believe he was Jesus Christ in a preincarnate appearance on the earth.
3. Some believe that he was an ancient king who was a type of Jesus Christ ("like the Son of God").

The fact that he was without parents, genealogy, and so on, simply means that these facts are not recorded in the Old Testament record. I accept this third option, because it appears from the story that Melchizedek was a real human person who met Abram. He was an ancient king from the city of Salem who was a follower of the Most High God and was a type of Jesus Christ.

So What?

Scholars have tended to get bogged down in debate over the identity of Melchizedek. Rather than being absorbed by these discussions, let me suggest several practical lessons from this story of Abram and Melchizedek.

1. Some Pursue and Some Provide. "When Abram heard that his relative had been taken captive, he called out the 318 trained men born in his household and went in pursuit as far as Dan" (Genesis 14:14). Abram pursued his captive relative. Against all odds and at great personal sacrifice, Abram traveled 240 miles to wage war in order to liberate Lot. The lesson is obvious. When people are taken captive by sin, we have a responsibility to pursue and liberate (Galatians 6:1).

"Then Melchizedek king of Salem brought out bread and wine. He was priest of God Most High" (Genesis 14:18). Abram pursued. Melchizedek provided. Abram returns from war in a state of physical, mental, and emotional exhaustion. Melchizedek brings him bread and wine. This simple act does not appear to be of great spiritual significance, but it is. In the family of God there are those who wage war on the front lines. They live in the trenches of human despair. Against all odds they are in the business of liberating enslaved people. It's a tough and exhausting business. Thank God for others in the body who support the front-line soldiers. They meet us. They encourage us. They provide for us. They bless us. And the body of Christ needs both—pursuers and providers.

I have several Melchizedeks in my own life. One of them stops by my office on a regular basis. We talk together about the battle. He doesn't stay long, but before he leaves, he always says, "Let me pray for you." Much of my pastoral ministry is praying for others. Do you know what it feels like for someone to pray for me? My Melchizedek often enters my life when I'm on the way back from a demanding spiritual battle. Some pursue. Some provide.

2. We Give the Effort, God Gives the Victory. "And blessed be God Most High, who delivered your enemies into your hand" (Genesis 14:20). Abram put a lot of effort into the defeat of the eastern kings and the liberation of Lot. But Melchizedek puts it all in perspective. Did Abram pursue? Yes! Did Abram fight? Yes! Did Abram get the victory? No! The victory came from God. The lesson is that we do what God wants us to do, but it is God alone who grants success. We may plant the seed. We may water the seed. But God gives the increase.

Ed Dobson is incapable of changing one person's life. And so are you. In fact, Ed Dobson is not responsible for how people respond to the message of the gospel. I often hear people say, "Well, I've kind of given up on that person. I've talked to him. I've prayed for him. I've met with him. He used to come to church. He used to be involved, but he has just gotten so far from God. Talking to him is like wasting my time." Ah, you have it all out of perspective. My obligation is to put arms of love and compassion around those who are hurting. I must pursue those who are struggling. I must find those who have wandered away. I must reach out to those who are held captive. It is my responsibility to pursue! But it is *God* who gives the *victory*.

3. God Has a People, and They Don't All Wear the Same Label. Think of the life of Abram up to this point. God comes to him and says, "Abram, you're my man. I'm going to give you this land. Your family will be great. I'm going to bless the world through you." So Abram follows God and believes this promise. Abram is surrounded by all sorts of pagan tribes and heathen cities. He walks around the land, thinking, *I'm it! God chose me. I'm not like all these other pagans. I'm special to God. There is nobody else who knows God.*

Then one day he bumps into Melchizedek—a king from a pagan city. And he is the priest of El Elyon. Abram must have been shocked. He discovered he was not the *only* one who worshiped El Elyon. Abram discovered that God had a people, and they didn't all wear the same label.

The same is true today. God has faithful people and they don't all wear the same label. They are not all Baptists—thank God. They are not all Presbyterians—amen. They are not all Catholics—hallelujah. And the list goes on!

I thank God for my distinctive religious background. I grew up with the Plymouth Brethren, then I joined a Bible church. I was ordained into the Baptist movement. I came to Grand Rapids to a nondenominational church. I need to be reminded that there are many other people who love God who don't wear my labels. There are times when we ought to stop and realize that while we wander around thinking we're the only ones, we would be absolutely surprised to know that God has a people bigger than us. And they don't all have the same label!

Growing up in the Plymouth Brethren in Northern Ireland, we had a popular joke among ourselves. "When you get to heaven, and you see this little group over in the corner, walk by really quietly. It's the Plymouth Brethren, and they think they are the only ones up there!" What a joy and delight to see in Genesis 14 that God has a people, and they don't all wear the same label.

Prayer

Father, for those who have been taken captive, help them to know that your love has pursued them all the way. For those who have been pursuing and are about to give up, help them to realize that we pursue, but you give the victory. For those who need a Melchizedek, and encourager, I pray that you would encourage them with your presence, with your word, with your spirit, with your promises. Bring someone into their lives to offer a cup of cold water in Jesus' name. Thank you for the lessons that we can learn from very real people struggling with the issues of trusting you. And thank you for every believer who loves you—whatever his or her label. In Jesus' name I pray. Amen.

Chapter Six

Faith in the Face of the Impossible

Got any rivers you think are uncrossable?
Got any mountains you can't tunnel through?
God specializes in things tho't impossible
He does the things others cannot do.

OSCAR ELIASON

Easy to sing. Hard to live. Trusting God in the face of impossibility is not easy to do. It's a lot easier to trust him when things are going well: when the business is up, when all the kids are healthy, when you've just passed your annual physical, when all of the bills are paid, when there is no sickness in your immediate family, when you enjoy coming to church, and when you enjoy serving the Lord. When everything falls in place, it doesn't take a lot of faith to trust God. But God often brings us to the uncrossable mountain and asks us, "Will you trust me now?" This is precisely where we find Abram in Genesis 15.

The chapter begins with two words: "After this." What happens in this chapter follows the intensity of the events in chapter 14. Abram had just returned from victory over the eastern kings. He had met Melchizedek and received a blessing. He had given a tenth of his possessions to Melchizedek. Abram is on a high.

Notice what God says to him following his victory:

> "Do not be afraid Abram.
> I am your shield,
> Your very great reward."

This is a puzzling statement. Why would Abram be afraid? He had just defeated an alliance of eastern kings. He was a war hero. The battle was over. Yet at this exact moment God says, "Don't be afraid." Why?

Although Abram was on top of the world outwardly, he was struggling with incredible inward defeat. God had promised him a son, but he had none. Childless couples will understand this pain of Abram. All the victories in the world, all the goods in the world, all the tents in the world, all the possessions in the world, all the status in the world in no way compares to one son. Abram would have gladly given up the victories, the houses, his status, the lands, if he could only have had one son.

So in spite of the success, an ache fills Abram's heart. What he longs for most and what he has been promised by God has not been fulfilled, and he is now an old man. In Abram's moment of despair, God appears to him and says, "Don't be afraid, don't worry about a son." This is a good reminder for us not to judge people by outward appearance of success. Beneath the homes, lands, titles, and properties there is often an aching and broken heart. I recently talked to a good friend. He is the epitome of corporate success. He runs major corporations in various countries around the world. He travels over 200,000 miles each year. He rides in chauffeur-driven cars and limousines. He enjoys the perks of sitting at the top. But he carries the pain of a wayward son and a broken marriage. I ache for him and have recommitted myself to more constant prayer and encouragement on his behalf.

Abram responds to God by stating his pain: "But Abram said, 'O Sovereign LORD, what can you give me since I remain childless and the one who will inherit my estate is Eliezer of Damascus?'" (Genesis 15:2).

I like Abram. He gets to the bottom line. Abram is not interested in theoretical promises floating around in the air. In fact, he has figured out a few options on his own, in case God does not come through. The custom of the land is that if you don't have an heir, the eldest servant in your household automatically inherits all the possessions.

Abram talks to God. "So God, while you're telling me about all those promises and all this theory, that's fine. But I want to know, bottom line, how is this going to work out? How is it going to happen?"

Notice the Lord's response: "Then the word of the LORD came to him: 'This man will not be your heir, but a son coming from your own body will be your heir'" (Genesis 15:4). God is pushing Abram to the brink of faith.

Abram says, "Okay, you're the sovereign God, and you made this promise. The only problem is, it's impossible. I really want to believe your promise, so I have an alternative." The alternative is Eliezer of Damascus.

God says, "No, no, Abram. I made you a promise, and I intend to keep it. The promise is *You will have a son*."

Now can you imagine Abram? He really wants to trust God.

God has a delightful sense of humor. Notice what he does. "He took him outside and said, 'Look up to the heavens and count the stars—if indeed you can count them.' Then he said to him. 'So shall your offspring be'" (Genesis 15:5). Now all Abram wanted was one son—just one! God said, "You're going to have him. In fact, let me give you an object lesson. Let me show you what's going to happen. Even though you are facing the impossible, even though I'm stretching your faith, look up at the stars. That's what your offspring is going to be like."

Abram is old. His wife is beyond the age of childbearing. Having a son is impossible. I wonder what Abram thought. Maybe, *Give me a break, God. I want one child—not millions.* Whatever he thought, he did respond appropriately. "And [Abram] believed, (trusted in, relied on, remained steadfast to the Lord); and He counted it to him as righteousness [right standing with God]" (Genesis 15:6 AMP).

You Have to Get to First Base Before You Can Get to Second

Abram is standing at the plate in shock. He has just struck out. Yet God tells him, "You will get to first base—you will have a son." Abram knows he has tried and failed. He knows he and Sarai are too old. He is out! But God says, "You'll get to first." As Abram stands there, trying to process all this, God adds, "And by the way, you'll also get to second base." "He also said to him, 'I am the LORD, who brought you out of Ur of the Chaldeans to give you this land to take possession of it'" (Genesis 15:7).

Now put yourself in Abram's place for just a moment. God says Abram's going to have a son, even though that is a biological impossibility. Abram says, "Okay, God, I believe you." God says, "Now that you really trust me, let me give you part two of the plan. I'm not only going to give you a son; I am also going to give you this land." Now Abram is fully aware that he does not possess the land. In fact look at the last verse of the chapter, notice who's in control. It is the land of the Kenites, Kenizzites, Kadmonites, Hittites, Perizzites, Rephaites, Amorites, Canaanites, Girgashites, and Jebusites. God says, "I'm not only going to give you a son, I'm going to give you the land." Abram is fully aware that he is a long way from possessing the land. Abram is just like us. He said, "Okay God, if that's what you're going to give me, how are you going to do it?" Scripture states that "Abram said, 'O

Sovereign LORD, how can I know that I will gain possession of it?'" (Genesis 15:8). The answer God gave is filled with deep significance and symbolism.

Have I Got a Deal for You!

So the LORD said to him, "Bring me a heifer, a goat and a ram, each three years old, along with a dove and a young pigeon."

Abram brought all these to him, cut them in two and arranged the halves opposite each other; the birds, however, he did not cut in half.

Genesis 15:9, 10

The strange procedure described above is called the cutting of a covenant. A covenant is a legal contract between two parties in which each party binds himself to fulfill certain conditions and thereby receives certain promised advantages. In the Old Testament, when two people signed a legal document, it was called cutting a covenant (making or cutting a deal).

There were two kinds of covenants. One was a conditional covenant, an agreement between two people that was predicated on certain conditions. If you do this, then I will do that. If you don't do this, then I am free of the obligations of this agreement. That was a conditional covenant.

The second kind of covenant was unconditional. This agreement had no preconditions. Whatever each party did or said, the agreement was final and binding. They agreed, whatever the response of either party, that the agreement or the covenant stood. In ancient times, when two parties made a covenant, they did not call the local attorney to draft a document, because they didn't have attorneys. They were unable, therefore, to make a legal document, notarize the document, and sign it in the presence of witnesses. When two people made an agreement, they brought an animal or several animals. They cut them in half. They laid the pieces opposite each other in a row. Then the two people stood together, hand in hand, and walked down through the middle of the pieces. They pledged in the face of death and suffering that they would honor the agreement.

So Abram knows what God is doing. God is about to make an agreement with Abram. According to the customs of the land he arranges all the pieces of the sacrifice. When they make the deal, they will walk together, hand in hand, between the animals.

One of the ideas is that if one of them breaks the covenant, they will face death, like the animals around them. Jeremiah makes this point: "The men who have violated my covenant and have not fulfilled the terms of the covenant they made before me, I will treat like the calf they cut in two and then walked between its pieces" (Jeremiah 34:18). This was the general custom in the ancient world. If a person broke the covenant, he faced the ultimate penalty of death.

The stage is set for the cutting of a deal. Abram waits to walk with God between the pieces of the animals. But something strange happens:

> When the sun had set and darkness had fallen, a smoking fire-pot with a blazing torch appeared and passed between the pieces. On that day the LORD made a covenant with Abram and said, "To your descendants I give this land, from the river of Egypt to the great river, the Euphrates—the land of the Kenites, Kenizzites, Kadmonites, Hittites, Perizzites, Rephaites, Amorites, Canaanites, Girgashites and Jebusites."
>
> Genesis 15:17–21

The smoking firepot with a blazing torch represents the presence of God. This firepot passed between the pieces—*alone!* God walks between the pieces to finalize the legal agreement. What is the significance of this? It is that God is making an unconditional agreement with Abram.

He is not saying, "Now Abram, if you will live up to certain conditions, then you will have a son, and I will give you the land." He is not saying, "Abram, as long as you obey A, B, C, and D, I'll keep my end of the bargain."

God is saying to Abram, "I'm going to give you this land, and I am making an unconditional promise that you will receive it. It is not up to you, your effort, your battle strategy, your initiative, or your intelligence. You will get the land because I'm going to make it happen. I am making this agreement. I am passing through the pieces. I am making an agreement that you'll possess the land."

To this day and hour Israel has never fully possessed the land. If you study the Scriptures, God prophetically declares that one day they will. In God's timing they will, because as recorded in the fifteenth chapter of Genesis, God made a deal with Abram. God pledged his person, his character, and his power to that agreement. God personally passed between the pieces. I believe that what God promised to Abram one day will come to pass because God made a deal. God passed between the pieces. God said there are no conditions. If God fails to do it, he has broken his covenant. He has failed in his agreement.

The God of History

Then the LORD said to him, "Know for certain that your descendants will be strangers in a country not their own, and they will be enslaved and mistreated four hundred years. But I will punish the nation they serve as slaves, and afterward they will come out with great possessions. You, however, will go to your fathers in peace and be buried at a good old age. In the fourth generation your descendants will come back here, for the sin of the Amorites has not yet reached its full measure."

Genesis 15:13–16

The promises of God to Abram and his descendants were not without pain and struggle. In these verses God makes a seven-fold prophecy concerning the nations of Israel. All seven points were fulfilled.

1. You will be strangers in another country (Egypt).
2. You will be slaves in that country.
3. You will be mistreated 400 years (the actual period of slavery was 430 years. In this passage it is rounded off to 400).
4. God will punish Egypt.
5. Israel will be delivered with great possessions.
6. Abram will not live through this period of slavery.
7. In the fourth generation (400 years), Israel will return to the land.

You Can Be Sure That God Will Keep His Promises

One of the major lessons of this story is that God will keep his promises. People will let you down; it doesn't matter whether you sign a legal agreement. They'll still let you down. They'll still do what they want, when they want, when it is convenient. If your faith and your trust are in people, you're going to be disappointed. But God will not fail! You can trust his promise. God promised Abram a land over 4,000 years ago. When the promise was made, the land was filled with other tribes and nations. It was not Abram's land. It was the land of the "Kenites, Kenizzites, Kadmonites, Hittites, Perizzites, Rephaites, Amorites, Canaanites, Girgashites and Jebusites." Over 4,000 years have passed.

The Jews continue to exist as a people, and they possess the land. Where are the Kenites, Kenizzites, Kadmonites, Hittites, Perizzites, Rephaites, Amonites, Canaanites, Girgashites, and Jebusites? They've disappeared. Where are the Jews? All over the world and in the land. Why? Because God keeps his promise.

Paul Johnson, in his book *A History of the Jews* (Harper-Collins, 1987), observes this phenomenon of the continued existence of the Jews and their connection to Palestine. He describes the importance of Hebron—the ancient burial site of Abram and the patriarchs—and its 4,000-year history. After identifying the many nations who have conquered and controlled this site, he concludes:

> So when the historian visits Hebron today, he asks himself: where are all those peoples which once held the place? Where are the Canaanites? Where are the Edomites? Where are the ancient Hellenes and the Romans, the Byzantines, the Franks, the Mamluks and the Ottomans? They have vanished into time, irrevocably. But the Jews are still in Hebron.
>
> Hebron is thus an example of Jewish obstinacy over 4,000 years. It also illustrates the curious ambivalence of the Jews towards the possession and occupation of land. No race has maintained over so long a period so emotional an attachment to a particular corner of the earth's surface. But none has shown so strong and persistent an instinct to migrate, such courage and skill in pulling up then replanting its roots. It is a curious fact that, for more than three-quarters of their existence as a race, a majority of Jews have always lived outside the land they call their own. They do so today.

The God who has been faithful to his promise to Abram for 4,000 years is faithful to *all* his promises to us. You can trust him.

You Cannot Trust All God's Promises

While God is trustworthy, you better not trust all his promises. There is a little chorus that says, "Every promise in the book is mine—every chapter, every verse, every line." Wrong! That is terrible theology. Not *every* promise in this book is mine. God just made a promise to Abram. Abram would have a son in his old age. That has nothing to do with me, when I am old. God made another promise to Abram: "I'm going to give you this land, and you will possess it." That promise has absolutely nothing to do with me. It's not for me!

When you claim God's promises, there are two questions you must ask. First, *Is the promise for me?* I know people who take these promises of possessing the land, and they declare that as a church God wants them to have a piece of property. They claim it for God—based on these promises! Now God may want you to have it. God may be leading you to get it. But don't claim a promise that wasn't for you in the first place.

Second, ask, *Is the promise conditional or unconditional?* If the promise is for me, do I have to meet certain conditions, and *then* God will fulfill his promise? Or is this promise unconditional? Does God say, "This is what I am going to do for you. I am passing down between the pieces myself. I am committing my character and power and person to this. I'm going to do it."

Let me show you the difference. Let us look at two promises in Philippians. The first is unconditional: "Being confident of this, that he who began a good work in you will carry it on to completion until the day of Christ Jesus" (Philippians 1:6).

God did not say, "If you are a Baptist, then I will complete the work of salvation." He did not say, "If you don't smoke or chew or mess around, I will complete the work of salvation." God didn't say that. He made an unconditional promise. "I started the work of salvation. What I started in you, I will bring to completion. It does not depend on you." So I know, in spite of my failures and sins and mistakes, I have an unconditional promise. The God who began a work of salvation in my life carries that work on to completion. This is called the assurance of my salvation. It's unconditional.

The second promise is conditional. "And my God will meet all your needs according to his glorious riches in Christ Jesus" (Philippians 4:19). We all have this verse memorized. What a glorious promise! God will supply all of our needs according to his riches in glory by Christ Jesus. Notice the first word of the promise: *and*. What kind of a word is it? It is a conjunction. What does a conjunction do? It connects. Here is a promise, but it is not unconditional, God is not saying in this verse, "I pass through the pieces. It doesn't matter how you live. It doesn't matter what you do. It doesn't matter what a mess your life is in. I'll always supply all of your needs." It does not apply to the person who ran up all of his credit cards to the limit. He got in debt and claimed, "My God will supply all of my need according to his riches in glory by Christ Jesus."

This promise is connected to a principle, the principle of giving.

Yet it was good of you to share in my troubles. Moreover, as you Philippians know, in the early days of your acquaintance with the gospel, when I set out from Macedonia, not one church shared with me in the matter of giving and receiving, except you only; for even when I was in Thessalonica, you sent me aid again and again when I was in need. Not that I am looking for a gift, but I am looking for what may be credited to your account. I have received full payment and even more; I am amply supplied, now that I have received from Epaphroditus the gifts you sent. They are a fragrant offering, an acceptable sacrifice, pleasing to God.

Philippians 4:14–18

Paul is commending the church as a giving church. Again and again they gave of their financial and material resources to meet Paul's need. In fact, Paul had everything he needed because of their love and generosity. Therefore, Paul gives them the promise of God. "*And* my God will supply *your* need."

They regularly gave to the needs of others; therefore God would meet their need.

You want to claim this promise? Give! You want to miss the promise? Be selfish! Hoard what you have. Hang on to what you own. Then you will never know the blessing of the benefits of God's resources. If you'll take what God has given you, let it go. If you will give again and again and again, the promise is this: For those who give, God will supply *all* your need according to his riches in glory by Christ Jesus.

Isn't that a wonderful promise? We can't outgive God! We get so protective and possessive of what we have. But we just can't outgive God. If we will give and give and give and give, Paul says, God has a simple promise that is based on the giving spirit: My God *will* supply, not some, *all* of our needs, according to his riches in glory by Christ Jesus.

Trusting the Promise of God Is Not Easy

It is one thing to read and understand God's promises; it is another thing to trust them. In this story you not only learn about God and his promises, you also learn about Abram's struggle to believe those promises. In fact, it provides at least three important insights.

1. Faith Is Trusting God's Timing—Not Your Own. In this story Abram twice addresses God as "O Sovereign LORD" (vv. 2, 8). The sovereignty of God simply means that he is in control of the events of human history. Abram believed that. But he had a hard time fitting it into his human timetable. Did Abram ever have a son? Yes! On Abram's schedule? No! In Abram's timetable? No! Oftentimes we trust God for Eastern Standard Time, when he is operating on Pacific Coast Time. God's timing and ours often do not meet. Faith means we trust the timing of God, not our own.

We tend to set ultimatums. "Well, God, I must have it, and I must have it by such-and-such a date." You know what happens? Sometimes God does it by such-and-such a date, but sometimes the date passes. Then another date passes and another month passes and another year passes and our faith is stretched, tested. We find ourselves discouraged.

Faith is trusting God's timing. The issue is this: Is God in control, or is he not in control? If God is in control, he is never early; he is never late. He is always right on time. Have you ever noticed in the Bible how often it says "when the fullness of time was come"—God always operates on schedule. His on-time-arrival schedule is perfect. Never early. Never late. He never forgets and is always on time.

2. Faith Is Trusting God in Spite of Your Circumstances. Faith is trusting God when everything within you resists. Faith is saying, "God I know you are in control. I know you are on time. I know that these are impossible circumstances." Faith is trusting God in spite of your circumstances; doubt is trusting your circumstances in spite of God.

The Bible is a book full of promises. Not one of them has ever failed. The Bible is filled with the lives of real people like you and me. People who struggled, who prayed, who trusted God, who faced the impossible. God never failed one of them! And he will not fail you.

3. Faith Is Obeying God, One Step at a Time. "So the LORD said to him, 'Bring me a heifer, a goat and a ram, each three years old, along with a dove and a young pigeon'" (Genesis 15:9). God made a simple request. "Get a heifer, a goat, a ram, a dove, and a pigeon." What in the world does that have to do with getting a son? We find ourselves at point A, and we need to get to point B. You know what we try to do? We try to take one giant step, all at once, and we usually fail. God said, "Abram for you to get from here to here, you need to get the heifer, the goat, the ram, the dove, and the pigeon." So Abram brought all these to the Lord. Overcoming the mountain of despair begins by taking one small step of obedience. Faith means facing the impossible, the difficult, the stresses and challenges of life. It is determining by the grace of God that we will trust God for the impossible. The next step is to obey God. It means I may still struggle, but I'll never stop obeying God. I'll keep reading his Word. I'll keep praying. I'll keep in the fellowship of saints. I'll keep living in obedience to God. I will move forward one little step of obedience at a time.

You know what doubt is? Saying, "God, I can't face those circumstances. I'm not sure that you are able to make a difference. So I'm not going to live for you. I'm not going to read the Bible. I'm not going to pray. I'm not going to serve others. I'm not going to do the things I know I ought to do. I'm just going to wrap myself in the garments of self-pity and sit here and be miserable until it gets better."

Faith says, "I hurt. I struggle. I even doubt. But by your grace and with your help I'm going to keep on walking. I'm going to keep on living. I'm going to keep on praying. I'm going to keep on trusting one step, one moment, one day at a time! Then one day I'll look back and simply say, "Jesus led me all the way."

Prayer

Father, teach us to trust your timing, not our own. Teach us to trust you in spite of the circumstances. Teach us to move forward in simple steps of obedience. For those who hurt, encourage them. For those who face what Abram did, may they find you as their sovereign Lord. Encourage us. Help us to walk by faith and not by sight. For we ask it in Jesus' name and for his glory. Amen.

Chapter Seven

I Can Do It on My Own

Spiritual failure often follows on the heels of spiritual success. We come down from mountaintop experiences and fall flat on our faces. Look at Elijah. One day he stands on Mount Carmel and calls down fire from heaven. With incredible courage he opposes the forces of evil and the prophets of Baal. The next day he runs away from Jezebel, who declares she will have him killed. Elijah falls from the height of courage to the depths of fear in twenty-four hours. Beware of success, because failure may lie just ahead.

In the previous chapter Abram was on the mountaintop. God appeared to him in a vision and confirmed his unconditional covenant with Abram. God promised Abram a son through Sarai as well as the land of Palestine. God said, "Do not be afraid, Abram. I am your shield, your very great reward" (Genesis 15:1). Following this significant experience of God's presence and promise, Abram falls into the depths of despair by taking matters into his own hands.

Now Sarai, Abram's wife, had borne him no children. But she had an Egyptian maidservant named Hagar; so she said to Abram, "The Lord has kept me from having children. Go, sleep with my maidservant; perhaps I can build a family through her."

Abram agreed to what Sarai said. So after Abram had been living in Canaan ten years, Sarai his wife took her Egyptian maidservant Hagar and gave her to her husband to be his wife.

Genesis 16:1–3

Before we study the rest of the story, there is a dramatic contrast between the previous chapter and this chapter. In chapter 15 one of the key elements is the voice of God and Abram's response to it. In contrast, one of the key thoughts in chapter 16 is the voice of Sarai and Abram's response to it.

After this, the word of the LORD came to Abram (15:1).
Then the word of the LORD came to him (15:4).
He [the Lord] also said to him (15:7).
So the LORD said to him (15:9).
Then the LORD said to him (15:13).

Throughout chapter 15, God is speaking, and Abram is listening and responding in faith.

So she said to Abram (16:2).
Then Sarai said to Abram (16:5).

In chapter 16 Abram listens to the voice of his wife and ignores what God has already told him. For Abram, this was the beginning of failure.

The same is true in our lives. When we pay more attention to the voices of human beings than to the voice of God, we are setting the stage for spiritual failure. Ignoring God and working problems out on our own only makes a bad situation worse. The consequences of ignoring God are serious and devastating. When I operate in the flesh, when I think in the flesh, when I speak in the flesh, when I respond in the flesh, when I move in the flesh, and when I walk in the flesh, I am destined for failure (Galatians 6:7, 8).

Abram tried to work it out on his own, and the situation *did* get worse.

He slept with Hagar, and she conceived.

When she knew she was pregnant, she began to despise her mistress. Then Sarai said to Abram. "You are responsible for the wrong I am suffering. I put my servant in your arms, and now that she knows she is pregnant, she despises me. May the LORD judge between you and me."

"Your servant is in your hands," Abram said. "Do with her whatever you think best." Then Sarai mistreated Hagar; so she fled from her.

Genesis 16:4–6

Notice that in Abram's fleshly choice, there are six serious consequences.

1. Hagar Despised Sarai. "He slept with Hagar, and she conceived. When she knew she was pregnant, she began to despise her mistress" (Genesis 16:4).

2. Blame Someone Else. "Then Sarai said to Abram, 'You are responsible for the wrong I am suffering. I put my servant in your arms, and now that she knows she is pregnant, she despises me. May the LORD judge between you and me'" (Genesis 16:5).

Having an heir (son) through Hagar was Sarai's idea (v. 2). Abram followed her suggestion. Now Sarai encounters negative consequences and immediately reacts by blaming Abram. Have you ever done that? You made a wrong decision. You operated in the flesh. You went against God. You start to suffer the consequences. What do you do? Blame somebody else!

3. Get Spiritual. "Then Sarai said to Abram, 'You are responsible for the wrong I am suffering. I put my servant in your arms, and now that she knows she is pregnant, she despises me. May the LORD judge between you and me'" (Genesis 16:5).

Now Sarai brings God into it, as if somehow God is accountable and responsible. "May the LORD judge between you and me." That's just what we do when we mess up. We blame somebody else; then we blame God.

4. It's Not My Problem, It's Yours. "'Your servant is in your hands,' Abram said. 'Do with her whatever you think best.'" (Genesis 16:6).

Sarai says to Abram, "It's your fault. You're the one who brought all this about."

Abram says, "It's not *my* fault." Now it really is: He is the father of the child conceived in the womb of Hagar. It's really as much his fault as it is Sarai's fault. But neither of them wants to accept the blame.

Abram says, "It's not my problem, she's your servant. You do what you think best." One of the consequences of failure is that we hesitate to accept our personal responsibility for bringing about the failure. We tend to pass the bulk of the responsibility to anyone or everyone else.

5. Sarai Mistreated Hagar. "Then Sarai mistreated Hagar" (Genesis 16:6).

When we fail to accept responsibility for our bad decisions, we tend not only to blame others, but to hurt others. Failure to trust and obey God affects us and those around us. Others may get mistreated.

6. Hagar Ran Away. "So she [Hagar] fled from her [Sarai]" (Genesis 16:6).

In this story Hagar is primarily a victim of the decisions of Sarai and Abram. As a slave, she had no right to refuse her owners. Abram and Sarai bear the full responsibility for their decision. Yet Hagar is mistreated and runs away. It is usually the victims of the sinful decisions of others who suffer the most deeply.

Problems multiply when you make wrong decisions. We love to shift the blame from one person to the other. Then we shift it back to the first person and to God! When you make a bad decision and you do not deal with it properly, it keeps getting worse and worse!

You Cannot Run from God

The angel of the LORD found Hagar near a spring in the desert; it was the spring that is beside the road to Shur. And he said, "Hagar, servant of Sarai, where have you come from, and where are you going?"

"I'm running away from my mistress Sarai," she answered. Then the angel of the LORD told her, "Go back to your mistress and submit to her."

Genesis 16:7–9

The angel gives Hagar a strange piece of advice. "Go back to your mistress and submit to her." First a word of caution about what this does *not* mean. It does not mean that in a marital situation, if you are being physically abused, you ought to stay there and take the abuse. That's not what it means at all. The underlying principle being taught is that you cannot run to Egypt to avoid your problems. You cannot run away from them.

Have you ever discovered that wherever you run, your problems go with you? I often meet people who say, "Well, I'm going to leave that church and come to this church, because we are having all sorts of problems over there. If I could just get into a new environment and a new setting, then all of my problems would go away."

Wrong!

The advice of the angel is, "Don't run from your problems." Face them. The underlying promise is that God will see you through. In fact, the angel gave Hagar a promise:

The angel added, "I will so increase your descendants that they will be too numerous to count." The angel of the LORD also said to her: "You are now with child and you will have a son. You shall name him Ishmael, for the LORD has heard of your misery. He will be a wild donkey of a man; his hand will be against everyone and everyone's hand against him, and he will live in hostility toward all his brothers."

She gave this name to the LORD who spoke to her: "You are the God who sees me," for she said, "I have now seen the One who sees me." That is why the well was called Beer Lahai Roi; it is still there, between Kadesh and Bered. So Hagar bore Abram a son, and Abram gave the name Ishmael to the son she had borne. Abram was eighty-six years old when Hagar bore him Ishmael.

Genesis 16:10–16

Lessons from Failure

In this story of Abram's failure we discover three important lessons that teach us something about the nature of God, the nature of failure, and the nature of faith.

The Nature of God

The characteristics of the nature of God are obvious in this story. First, he is the God who sees. Second, he is the God who hears. Whenever we find ourselves driven out into the desert and overwhelmed with the adversity of our problems; when we find ourselves all alone; when we are not sure what we have left, and we are not certain where we are going, and all the problems are coming our way, remember the lesson of the character of God. God hears, and God sees. You are not walking alone. Your problems may seem overwhelming, but God hears and God sees.

The Nature of Failure

The failure story was twofold. First, Abram listened to the voice of human beings rather than to the voice of God. Whenever I pay more attention to what people think and what people say than to what God has already revealed, I'm headed for serious trouble.

Second, when I put into practice the plans of man and ignore the promise of God, I'm headed for failure. In other words, when I jump into a problem that seems overwhelming, and I figure out my own solution, ignoring the promise and the Word of God, I am headed for failure. My own strength, intellect, and ability are poor substitutes for the promise and power of God.

The Nature of Faith

The life of Abram is a continuing struggle to live by faith. His faith is constantly put to the test. In this story we discover three essential elements of faith.

1. Faith Is Trusting God in Spite of the Circumstances. God has promised Abram a son through his wife, Sarai. Sarai was already too old to have children. It was a biological impossibility. Yet God said it would happen. Faith means trusting God even when the circumstances dictate against it.

In Hebrews 11 we are introduced to this element of faith through people who trusted God in spite of their circumstances.

> And what more shall I say? I do not have time to tell about Gideon, Barak, Samson, Jephthah, David, Samuel and the prophets, who . . . quenched the fury of the flames, and escaped the edge of the sword; whose weakness was turned to strength; and who became powerful in battle and routed foreign armies.
>
> Hebrews 11:32–34

In other words, some of them saw God intervene in miraculous ways, and the dead were raised. Others were tortured and refused to be released, awaiting a better resurrection. Some were tortured to death, but they still trusted God. "Some faced jeers and flogging, while still others were chained and put in prison" (Hebrews 11:36).

Trusting God in spite of the circumstances. Persecuted. Mis-treated. Driven from civilization. Despised. Destitute. Beaten. Imprisoned. Flogged. Burned. Beheaded. And they still trusted God! We know little about trusting God in spite of the circum-stances. To us, persecution occurs when the car won't start and we're late for church. In our society, persecution means incon-venience. But the history of the church and the history of God's people is that in the face of death itself they still trusted God.

In your life and mine, faith means hanging onto God and trust-ing his promises, whatever the circumstances. Whatever the dif-ficulty, whatever the opposition, whatever the persecution, I am still trusting God.

2. Faith Is Trusting God in Spite of the Delay. Abram expected an immediate response from God in giving him a son. When God delayed, Abram decided to help God out and made a mess of his family. Faith requires patience and trust, when God does not oper-ate on our time schedule.

3. Faith Is Trusting God on His Terms, Not Our Own. Abram wanted an heir on his terms (through Hagar) and ignored God's plan (through Sarai) (Hebrews 6:12). Faith is trusting God on his terms as well as his timetable. This is amplified in Romans 11:33–36:

> Oh, the depth of the riches of the wisdom and knowledge of God!
>> How unsearchable his judgments,
>> and his paths beyond tracing out!
> "Who has known the mind of the Lord?
>> Or who has been his counselor?"
> "Who has ever given to God, that God should repay him?"
> For from him and through him and to him are all things.
>> To him be the glory forever!
>> Amen.

You know what Paul is saying in the first verse? The wisdom of God is so infinitely superior to our wisdom, that we don't really fully understand it! The paths of God, the working of God, and the direction of God, cannot even be traced from a human point of view. Why? "Who has known the mind of the Lord?" (v. 34). Are we presumptuous enough to conclude that we know what God is doing? Are we arrogant enough to assume that we understand God's mind? Surely not!

"Who has been his counselor?" (v. 34). Are we chief counsel to the Almighty? No!

"Who has ever given to God, that God should repay him?" (v. 35). Is the Creator indebted to the creature? No! Here's faith. When you don't understand the ways of God, and you don't understand the wisdom of God, and when you don't understand the knowledge of God, and when you don't understand the mind of God, and you don't understand the judgment of God, faith is recognizing "for from him and through him and to him are *all* things" (v. 36, *italics added*). Does that include what you are facing now? Yes! For from and through and to him are *all* things. And what a footnote! "To him be the glory forever! Amen" (v. 36).

You see, in the final analysis God does what he wants, when he wants, and how he wants. Faith is trusting God in spite of our circumstances. It is trusting God in spite of the delay. It is trusting God on his terms, not our own.

Prayer

Father, we acknowledge by faith that your ways are beyond our ways. Your judgment and wisdom are beyond our understanding. We are not your counselor. We do not know your mind, other than what you have revealed through your Word. So we acknowledge that from you, through you, and unto you are all things.

We pray for those who are struggling like Hagar. We pray for those who are victims of the abuse of others. May they see your character and your presence. We pray for those who, like Sarai and Abram, have made bad decisions and are now shifting the blame.

We pray that you would help each of us to acknowledge when we sin. Help us not to run away from our problems, but to face them in your power and with your promise and help.

We know from experience, Lord, the frustration of failure. We know, not only from the life of Abram, but in our own personal lives how easy it is to operate in the arm of the flesh. We ask that you would help us to trust you, whatever our circumstances. Help us to trust you, whatever the delay. Help us to trust you on your terms, not our own. Thank you, Lord, that you are eternally trustworthy and that you will not fail.

Encourage each of us to walk by faith and not by sight.

In Jesus' name we pray. Amen.

Chapter Eight

When God Delays

> He is able, He is able
> I know he is able
> I know my Lord is able
> To carry me through.

Did you sing this chorus in Sunday school? I did—with enthusiasm. Although the words are simple, the truth is profound. God is able! But translating the reality of God's ability into the reality of our present need is a different matter. We know that God is able, whatever the circumstance, whatever the difficulty, whatever the problem. But often God does not come through on time. He delays, and we wonder if he *is* really able. This is the struggle of Abram. God had promised him a son. Yet God delays in following through. In fact, God had been making this promise for twenty-four years with *no* results.

Waiting for God Will Test Your Faith

When Abram was ninety-nine years old, the LORD appeared to him and said, "I am God Almighty; walk before me and be blameless. I will confirm my covenant between me and you and will greatly increase your numbers."

Genesis 17:1, 2

Notice this chapter in Genesis begins by giving us Abram's age—ninety-nine. In studying the life of Abram, we are given his age at various stages of his pilgrimage.

1. His Call. "So, Abram left, as the LORD had told him; and Lot went with him. Abram was seventy-five years old when he set out from Haran" (Genesis 12:4). Abram was seventy-five years old when he obeyed the call of God. He left his country, family, and friends. He followed God.

2. His Pilgrimage. "So after Abram had been living in Canaan ten years, Sarai his wife took her Egyptian maidservant Hagar and gave her to her husband to be his wife" (Genesis 16:3). During his pilgrimage, God makes two basic promises to Abram. First, he will be given the land of Palestine. Second, he will be given a son.

3. The Affirmation of God's Promise. "When Abram was ninety-nine years old, the LORD appeared to him and said, 'I am God Almighty; walk before me and be blameless. I will confirm my covenant between me and you and will greatly increase your numbers'" (Genesis 17:1, 2).

Abram began following God at age seventy-five. He is now ninety-nine. He has been following God for twenty-four years. During these years God has repeatedly told him that he will have a son and he will possess the land. After twenty-four years, what does Abram have to show for it? *Nothing*! He does not possess the land. He does not have a son. And twenty-four years have gone by. He and Sarai keep getting older.

At this point in Abram's life, God appears to him and says, "I am God Almighty [*El Shaddai*]." We are not told how Abram responded to God. If it had been me, I would have been rather cynical! "If you are God Almighty, what about the land? What about the son? You promised me both twenty-four years ago. And so far, nothing. If you are God Almighty, why can't you do something—now?"

Responding to the Delay of God

How do I respond to the delays of God? Notice that God gives Abram instructions. He tells Abram to do two things: walk before me and be blameless (Genesis 17:1).

The Walk

Walking before the Lord means living our lives with a constant awareness of God's presence. It implies that we are accountable to God, and we should seek to please him. It doesn't matter what others think—walk before God. It doesn't matter that you do not have a son—walk before God. It doesn't matter that the land is not in your possession—walk before God. It doesn't matter that God has delayed for twenty-four years—walk before God. We do not control God or his timing. God is God. Our responsibility is to walk before him. The Bible has much to say about our walk before God.

1. We Are to Walk with *God.* "Enoch walked with God; then he was no more, because God took him away" (Genesis 5:24). Walking with God means walking in harmony with him. It means to walk in step with him.

2. We Are to Walk after *God.* "Ye shall walk after the LORD your God, and fear him, and keep his commandments, and obey his voice, and ye shall serve him, and cleave unto him." (Deuteronomy 13:4 KJV).

What does it mean to walk after the Lord?

1. It means to fear him.
2. It means to keep his commandments.
3. It means to obey his voice.
4. It means to serve him.
5. It means to cleave to him.

We are to walk *before* the Lord in a constant awareness of his presence. We are to walk *with* the Lord in step with him, and we are to walk *after* the Lord by obeying him, serving him, following him, cleaving to him, and submitting to him.

3. We Are to Walk in *God.* So then, just as you received Christ Jesus as Lord, continue to live in him (Colossians 2:6). The word translated "to live" is the Greek verb *peripateo*. It means to "walk around." The text says that we are to walk around "in Jesus." It means to walk around in the love, character, and attitude of Jesus Christ. So what is the walk of the believer? It means to walk *before* him, realizing that in the final analysis the only thing that matters is what God thinks. It means walking *with* him. Walking in step with him and in harmony with him. It means walking *after* him. Whatever he wants and desires, we do! It means to walk *in* him. To walk each day in our community, in our home, in our business, surrounded by the love of Jesus Christ.

The Character

When God delays, our second response should be a commitment to live blamelessly (uprightly). The delay of God is no excuse for sin and disobedience. We must maintain our integrity before God while we await the fulfillment of his promises. When we wait in obedience, the blessing comes. Jesus told his disciples to wait in Jerusalem for the promise of the Holy Spirit. They waited and prayed, and the promise came.

> On one occasion, while he was eating with them, he gave them this command: "Do not leave Jerusalem, but wait for the gift my Father promised, which you have heard me speak about."
>
> When the day of Pentecost came, they were all together in one place. Suddenly a sound like the blowing of a violent wind came from heaven and filled the whole house where they were sitting.
>
> Acts 1:4; 2:1, 2

If we get tired of waiting and decide to do our own thing, the results are tragic. When God gave the Law to Israel, he brought Moses to the top of Mount Sinai. The people got tired of waiting for Moses to return, so they made a golden calf and worshiped it. God brought terrible judgment on Israel because they were unwilling to wait.

> When the people saw that Moses was so long in coming down from the mountain, they gathered around Aaron and said, "Come, make us gods who will go before us. As for this fellow Moses who brought us up out of Egypt, we don't know what has happened to him."
>
> Aaron answered them, "Take off the gold earrings that your wives, your sons and your daughters are wearing, and bring them to me."
>
> And the LORD struck the people with a plague because of what they did with the calf Aaron had made.
>
> Exodus 32:1, 2, 35

We do what we do. God does what he does. Our responsibility is to walk before God and be blameless. God's responsibility is to be true to his promise: "I will confirm my covenant between me and you and will greatly increase your numbers" (Genesis 17:2). The word *confirm* means "to set in motion." Abram could not set God's promise in motion. Only God could do that. God begins this process by changing Abram's name to *Abraham.*

> Abram fell facedown, and God said to him, "As for me, this is my covenant with you: You will be the father of many nations. No longer will you be called Abram; your name will be Abraham, for I have made you a father of many nations."
>
> Genesis 17:3–5

The name *Abram* means "exalted father." What a contradiction in terms, calling the man with no son an "exalted father." *Abraham* means "father of a multitude." This is an even greater contradiction in terms. For twenty-four years, Abram (exalted father) has been wandering around waiting for a son. Every time his name is called, it reminds him how hollow the promise sounds. Now he gets his family together and announces his new name. He is no longer *Abram* ("exalted father"). He is now *Abraham* ("father of a multitude").

I can hear one of the servants saying, "You've got to be kidding. What a joke! Abram is losing his mind. The desert sun is getting to him."

> I will make you very fruitful; I will make nations of you, and kings will come from you. I will establish my covenant as an everlasting covenant between me and you and your descendants after you for the generations to come, to be your God and the God of your descendants after you. The whole land of Canaan, where you are now an alien, I will give as an everlasting possession to you and your descendants after you; and I will be their God.
>
> Genesis 17:6–8

Notice the first two words of verse 6: "I will." These words occur five times in these verses.

1. I will make you very fruitful.
2. I will make nations of you.
3. I will establish my covenant.
4. I will give you the land as an everlasting possession.
5. I will be your God.

There is hope in the face of hopelessness. There is a way when you cannot see it. There is an answer when you do not have one.

The hope, the way, and the answer is God Almighty. I will. I will. I will. I will. I will.

> He is able, He is able
> I know He is able
> I know my Lord is able
> To carry you through.

The Sign of Commitment to God

Then God said to Abraham, "As for you, you must keep my covenant, you and your descendants after you for the generations to come. This is my covenant with you and your descendants after you, the covenant you are to keep: Every male among you shall be circumcised. You are to undergo circumcision, and it will be the sign of the covenant between me and you. For the generations to come every male among you who is eight days old must be circumcised, including those born in your household or bought with money from a foreigner—those who are not your offspring. Whether born in your household or bought with your money, they must be circumcised. My covenant in your flesh is to be an everlasting covenant."

Genesis 17:9–13

Circumcision was not a new practice. According to ancient literature, the Egyptians, the Edomites, the Ammonites, and the Moabites commonly practiced it. For the people of God, it outwardly expressed their allegiance to God and his covenant; it symbolized their faith. Faith in God cannot be confined to the inner recesses of the heart. It eventually finds outward expression. For a Christian these outward symbols of faith are varied. They include baptism as well as good works (James 2:14–19).

It's Okay to Laugh Before God

God also said to Abraham, "As for Sarai your wife, you are no longer to call her Sarai; her name will be Sarah. I will bless her and will surely give you a son by her. I will bless her so that she will be the mother of nations; kings of peoples will come from her."

Abraham fell facedown; he laughed and said to himself, "Will a son be born to a man a hundred years old? Will Sarah bear a child at the age of ninety?" And Abraham said to God, "If only Ishmael might live under your blessing!"

Genesis 17:15–18

If you were ninety-nine, and your wife was ninety, and God said you are going to have a son—you would burst out laughing, too.

How would you like to be a mother of a two-year-old at ninety-two years of age? Just think about that for a moment! A two-year-old! How would you like to be a hundred and eight when he got out of high school and a hundred and twelve when he got out of college?

No wonder Abraham laughed! He said, "God, You've got to be kidding!" It wasn't a disrespectful or cynical laugh. There are times in our spiritual experience where the only response is to laugh.

I remember when I was in college and God called me to preach. I laughed. I said, "God, you have got to be kidding. You have a wonderful sense of humor. You see, God, I don't even like getting up in speech class to give speeches. I don't like getting up in front of crowds. You have the wrong person." And I laughed. But when God sets out to accomplish something, he has the power to do it. He is *El Shaddai*, the Almighty God.

Just the Bottom Line, Please

Abraham has three basic questions for God.

1. What are you going to do?
2. How are you going to do it?
3. When are you going to do it?

Their conversation might have gone like this:

Abraham: "What are you going to do, God?"

God: "I'm going to give you a son."

Abraham: "Okay, God. How are you going to do it?"

God: "I'm going to do it through Sarah."

Abraham: "Unbelievable! When are you going to do it?"

God: "By this time next year."

Abraham: "Funniest thing I ever heard."

God answers all three questions:

> Then God said, "Yes, but your wife Sarah will bear you a son, and you will call him Isaac. I will establish my covenant with him as an everlasting covenant for his descendants after him. And as for Ishmael, I have heard you: I will surely bless him; I will make him fruitful and will greatly increase his numbers. He will be the father of twelve rulers, and I will make him into a great nation. But my covenant I will establish with Isaac, whom Sarah will bear to you by this time next year." When he had finished speaking with Abraham, God went up from him.
>
> Genesis 17:19–22

The name *Isaac* means "laughter." Every time Abraham calls his son Isaac, he will be reminded of this experience when he responded to God with laughter. In the next chapter we discover that Sarah also laughed at God's promise. But God got the last laugh. He gave them a son, as he had promised, and that child's name was "laughter."

Faith involves immediate obedience. Though Abraham hadn't seen the promised son, he acted as God had commanded. He wanted to keep his part of the covenant.

> On that very day Abraham took his son Ishmael and all those born in his household or bought with his money, every male in his household, and circumcised them, as God told him. Abraham was ninety-nine years old when he was circumcised, and his son Ishmael was thirteen; Abraham and his son Ishmael were both circumcised on that same day. And every male in Abraham's household, including those born in his household or bought from a foreigner, was circumcised with him.
>
> Genesis 17:23–27

Abraham did not hesitate to obey God. Even though God had delayed, Abraham knew that faith always demands obedience.

> Trust and obey, for there's no other way
> To be happy in Jesus,
> But to trust and obey.

Finding Hope for Today

> Against all hope, Abraham in hope believed and so became the father of many nations, just as it had been said to him, "So shall your offspring be." Without weakening in his faith, he faced the fact that his body was as good as dead—since he was about a hundred years old—and that Sarah's womb was also dead. Yet he did not waver through unbelief regarding the promise of God, but was strengthened in his faith and gave glory to God, being fully persuaded that God had power to do what he had promised.
>
> Romans 4:18–21

Here we discover new insight into the faith of Abraham. We see God's delay put into perspective.

Why does he delay in our lives? Sometimes God's opportunity does not come until our human extremity is reached. His opportunity to meet our need may not even begin until we have exhausted our own resources and all other options. His delay may be designed to bring us to a point where we recognize that there is no human hope—our only hope is God.

Abraham said, "My body is as good as dead. Sarah's womb is dead. There is no hope." But he was strengthened in his faith. He was fully persuaded that even though these were the circumstances, God had made a promise. The God who had made the promise had the power to do what he had promised.

Footnote on Hope

Psalm 107 is a wonderful passage of encouragement and hope. I recommend that you meditate on this psalm, which emphasizes the point that when we come to the end of our own resources, God is there to meet our need.

Our Hopelessness
Some wandered in desert wastelands, finding no way to a city where they could settle. They were hungry and thirsty, and their lives ebbed away.

vv. 4, 5

Our Hope
Then they cried out to the LORD in their trouble, and he delivered them from their distress. He led them by a straight way to a city where they could settle. Let them give thanks to the LORD for his unfailing love and his wonderful deeds for men, for he satisfies the thirsty and fills the hungry with good things.

vv. 6–9

Our Hopelessness

Some sat in darkness and the deepest gloom, prisoners suffer-ing in iron chains, for they had rebelled against the words of God and despised the counsel of the Most High. So he sub-jected them to bitter labor; they stumbled, and there was no one to help.

vv. 10–12

Our Hope

Then they cried to the LORD in their trouble, and he saved them from their distress. He brought them out of darkness and the deepest gloom and broke away their chains. Let them give thanks to the LORD for his unfailing love and his wonderful deeds for men, for he breaks down gates of bronze and cuts through bars of iron.

vv. 13–16

Our Hopelessness

Others went out to the sea in ships; there were merchants on the mighty waters. They saw the works of the LORD, his wonderful deeds in the deep. For he spoke and stirred up a tempest that lifted high the waves. They mounted up to the heavens and went down to the depths; in their peril their courage melted away. They reeled and staggered like drunken men; they were at their wits' end.

vv. 23–27

Our Hope

Then they cried out to the LORD in their trouble, and he brought them out of their distress. He stilled the storm to a whisper; the waves of the sea were hushed. They were glad when it grew calm, and he guided them to their desired haven. Let them give thanks to the LORD for his unfailing love and his wonder-ful deeds for men. Let them exalt him in the assembly of the people and praise him in the council of the elders.

vv. 28–32

Whoever is wise, let him heed these things and consider the great love of the LORD.

v. 43

Wherever you are you are not beyond the arms of unfailing love.

For I am convinced that neither death nor life, neither angels nor demons, neither the present nor the future, nor any powers, neither height nor depth, nor anything else in all creation, will be able to separate us from the love of God that is in Christ Jesus our Lord.

Romans 8:38, 39

Paul himself said, "Nothing shall separate us from the love of God that is in Christ Jesus." Why does God delay? Sometimes he delays so he can bring us into the most impossible of circumstances. The desert without a city—thirsty. Tossed about in the ocean. Nowhere to turn. At wits' end. We cry out to God in the depths of our distress. He delivers us. We experience his unfailing love.

Prayer

Father, remind us that you are the Almighty God. There is nothing too hard for you. You are the one who hears and answers. You deliver us from distress. Where there is no hope, you give hope. Where there is no way, you make a way. Where there is weariness, you give strength. Where there is thirst, you give water. Where there is hunger, you give food. Where there is no one to care, you care. So we give you thanks, because you do not fail. We pray especially for those who feel as if they've stumbled, and there is no one to care. They wander, and there is no direction. They're hungry, and there is no food. They are "at their wits' end." We pray, like Abraham, that against all hope they would trust you. May they know that you are the Almighty God and you delight in delivering through distress. Teach us, Lord, to trust you. Teach us to walk *before* you, to walk *with* you, to walk *after* you, and to walk *in* you. Our ultimate desire is to please you. In Jesus' name we pray. Amen.

Chapter Nine

If God Is in Control, Why Pray?

Frankly, some things in the Bible bother me—questions for which I do not have a fully satisfactory answer, the workings of God that defy a logical explanation. This chapter raises at least two of these troubling questions. First, how can a loving God destroy entire cities—including innocent children? This destruction seems rather primitive and vindictive, antithetical to the love and compassion of God. Second, if God is in control, why bother praying?

I am enough of a Calvinist to believe in the sovereignty of God. I am enough of an Arminian to believe in human responsibility. But reconciling the two seems impossible. If God is in control, he is going to do what he wants to do. Therefore, praying for his intervention is a senseless and useless activity. It's a waste of time.

Before we examine these questions in the context of this chapter, let us look at the story.

Sarah—Help!

The LORD appeared to Abraham near the great trees of Mamre while he was sitting at the entrance to his tent in the heat of the day. Abraham looked up and saw three men standing nearby. When he saw them, he hurried from the entrance of his tent to meet them and bowed low to the ground.

Genesis 18:1, 2

One of the three visitors who appeared to Abraham was God in a bodily form (we call this a theophany). The other two were angels in bodily form. When Abraham met them, he gave them a traditional greeting in the ancient world: He "bowed low to the ground." Although it is unlikely that Abraham knew one of these was God, he did recognize them as unusual visitors: "He said, 'If I have found favor in your eyes, my lord, do not pass your servant by'" (Genesis 18:3). He addressed one of them as "my lord." This was a common phrase of greeting when one addressed a person of higher rank or status.

Abraham invited them for a meal. I love the Scriptures' honesty. And one of the things that excites me about the life of Abraham is that God allows us to see the good, the bad, and the ugly. When I studied this story, I sat and laughed. Abraham is a lot like us. He makes commitments without talking to his wife.

In effect Abraham says, "Come on in, I'll wash your feet. I'll feed you a meal. Rest with us. I will take care of you." But he had nothing prepared for these unexpected guests. "So Abraham hurried into the tent to Sarah. 'Quick,' he said, 'Get three seahs of fine flour and knead it and bake some bread'" (Genesis 18:6).

"Don't ask me any questions Sarah," he might have said. "Don't give me the old lecture that I always overcommit myself. Let's not have a family discussion. I'm in a bind. Bail me out."

Like a wonderful loving wife, she does just that. "He then brought some curds and milk and the calf that had been prepared, and set these before them. When they ate, he stood near them under a tree" (Genesis 18:8).

More Laughter

"Where is your wife Sarah?" they asked him.
"There, in the tent," he said.

> Then the LORD said, "I will surely return to you about this time
> next year, and Sarah your wife will have a son."
>
> Genesis 18:9, 10

This promise of a son is one that God had given to Abraham
many times—without results. It sounds like the same broken
record. In the past, Abraham had responded to this promise by
raising objections with God or by offering alternatives to God's
plan. This time God adds a time schedule to his promise—one
year.

> Now Sarah was listening at the entrance to the tent, which was
> behind him. Abraham and Sarah *were already old* and well
> advanced in years, and Sarah was past the age of childbearing. So
> Sarah laughed to herself as she thought, "After I am *worn out* and
> my master is *old*, will I now have this pleasure?"
>
> Genesis 18:10–12, *italics added*

Abraham and Sarah were already old. That is an *understate-
ment*! Sarah is ninety. How would you like to be ninety when
these people show up at your condo in Florida to tell you that one
year from now you will give birth to a baby? No wonder Sarah
laughed. You recall that when God gave the promise to Abraham,
Abraham laughed. Now Sarah overhears the promise, and she
does the same thing.

> Then the LORD said to Abraham, "Why did Sarah laugh and
> say, 'Will I really have a child, now that I am old?' Is anything
> too hard for the LORD? I will return to you at the appointed time
> next year and Sarah will have a son."
>
> Sarah was afraid, so she lied and said, "I did not laugh." But he
> said, "Yes, you did laugh."
>
> Genesis 18:13–15

Poor Sarah. When confronted about her laughter, she denies it. I would, too. It's not nice to laugh at God.

In spite of her human response, God still keeps his promise. Abraham and Sarah's laughter does *not* force God to change his mind. God could have said, "Laugh at me? I'll find another couple who will take me seriously." But God did not do that. Even when we doubt his Word and laugh at his promises, he remains faithful.

> When the men got up to leave, they looked down toward Sodom, and Abraham walked along with them to see them on their way. Then the LORD said, "Shall I hide from Abraham what I am about to do? Abraham will surely become a great and powerful nation, and all nations on earth will be blessed through him. For I have chosen him, so that he will direct his children and his household after him to keep the way of the LORD by doing what is right and just, so that the LORD will bring about for Abraham what he has promised him."
>
> Genesis 18:16–19

God decides to inform Abraham of the impending judgment against Sodom. He wants Abraham to know and remember how God deals with nations. He wants Abraham to know that obedience brings blessing, and disobedience brings judgment. God communicates two important principles of judgment to Abraham.

1. God Keeps the Record. "Then the LORD said, 'The outcry against Sodom and Gomorrah is so great and their sin so grievous'" (Genesis 18:20). God keeps the record of sin and injustice. While sin may be ignored by others, it is never ignored by God. Sin cries out to him. It must be resolved.

We find this principle in other passages of Scripture:

> The LORD said, "What have you done? Listen! Your brother's blood cries out to me from the ground."
>
> Genesis 4:10

Look! The wages you failed to pay the workmen who mowed
our fields are crying out against you. The cries of the harvesters
have reached the ears of the Lord Almighty.

James 5:4

2. God Personally Observes the Sin. "I will go down and see if
what they have done is as bad as the outcry that has reached me.
If not, I will know" (Genesis 18:21). The Hebrew text literally
states, "I will go down personally and see if their sin is made
complete." Sin has been building up in Sodom. God has delayed
judgment because of his love and mercy. More sin builds up. Now
the cup of sin has been filled, and God moves in judgment. And he
does it personally. He does not send angels or other messengers.
He does not judge on what others report. He does not judge on
the observations of his assistants. He does it himself. He never
delegates the delicate matter of judgment.

Driving a Bargain with God

The next part of the narrative is an incredible story of Abraham arguing with God. He tries to talk God into sparing Sodom's
judgment.

Abraham's talk with God reminds me of many conversations
with my kids. When they want something, they chip away at my
resistance, until they get what they want. We finally reach a negotiated settlement.

"Dad, what time do I need to be home?"

"Eleven."

"Eleven? The movie doesn't get over till ten-thirty, and it's at
least thirty minutes to get home."

"Okay. Eleven-thirty."

"But we have to drop friends off on the way. That's another
fifteen minutes."

"All right! Eleven forty-five!"

"But we need to eat. I didn't have time to eat dinner, and we always go out to eat after a movie."

"Twelve-thirty! And that's final."

"Thanks, Dad."

Notice the parallel with Abraham's conversation in Genesis 18:22–32:

> The men turned away and went toward Sodom, but Abraham remained standing before the LORD. Then Abraham approached him and said: "Will you sweep away the righteous with the wicked? What if there are fifty righteous people in the city? Will you really sweep it away and not spare the place for the sake of the fifty righteous people in it? Far be it from you to do such a thing—to kill the righteous with the wicked, treating the righteous and the wicked alike. Far be it from you! Will not the judge of all the earth do right?
>
> The LORD said, "If I find fifty righteous people in the city of Sodom, I will spare the whole place for their sake."
>
> Then Abraham spoke up again: "Now that I have been so bold as to speak to the LORD, though I am nothing but dust and ashes, what if the number of the righteous is five less than fifty? Will you destroy the whole city because of five people?"
>
> "If I find forty-five there," he said, "I will not destroy it."
>
> Once again he spoke to him, "What if only forty are found there?"
>
> He said, "For the sake of forty, I will not do it."
>
> Then he said, "May the LORD not be angry, but let me speak. What if only thirty can be found there?" He answered, "I will not do it if I find thirty there."
>
> Abraham said, "Now that I have been so bold as to speak to the LORD, what if only twenty can be found there?"
>
> He said, "For the sake of twenty, I will not destroy it."
>
> Then he said, "May the LORD not be angry, but let me speak just once more. What if only ten can be found there?"

He answered, "For the sake of ten, I will not destroy it."

In examining this story we gain three insights into the way God deals with nations.

1. God Judges Sin. God not only judges personal sin, he judges national sin. Cries of sin and abuse ascend to God. When the cup of sin is complete, God personally judges those peoples.

2. God Delays Judgment When There Is a Righteous Influence on the Culture. Abraham said to the Lord, "Lord, if there are fifty righteous, would you spare the city for the benefit of the righteous influence on the culture?" God answered, "I will do it." Abraham drove the number down to forty-five, forty, thirty, twenty, and ten.

Now ultimately the city was destroyed, but not totally. Lot and his daughters escaped. Others had opportunity to escape. God agreed to spare the city from immediate and total judgment because of a righteous group within the city. It's the salt-and-light principle. We are the salt of the earth. We are the light of the world. In God's relationship with nations, God often spares his judgment of a nation because of the righteous influence of those living there.

3. God Delays Judgment When People Pray. God agreed to spare Sodom as a direct result of Abraham's intercession. We, too, can delay God's judgment upon nations by interceding for them before God.

If my people, who are called by my name, will humble themselves and pray and seek my face and turn from their wicked ways, then will I hear from heaven and will forgive their sin and will heal their land.

2 Chronicles 7:14

How Can a Loving God Destroy Entire Cities?

We now return to this troubling question of God's judgment. How could a loving God zap entire cities? How could a loving God destroy entire cultures—including little children? This is an often repeated moral issue in the Old Testament. While no completely satisfactory answer exists, we must keep in mind two principles from the story of Sodom.

God Is Long-suffering

God did not zap Sodom at the first hint of sin. Rather, he was patient with them. He gave them many opportunities to repent. Before he judged them, three things happened.

1. He Placed in That City a Personal Witness to His Righteousness—A man named Lot acted as God's witness. Whether or not Lot *should* have lived in the city is a moot question. The fact is that he did. Lot's righteous soul was in anguish every day because of the people's sin. In fact, Lot had enough influence in Sodom to become one of the political leaders of the city.

2. There Was a Filling of the Cup of Sin. The first time they sinned, God did not wipe them out. But over a long period of time as the sin grew and the cry of the sin ascended to God, there came a point in the plan of God where the cup of their iniquity was full. After God delayed repeatedly, he moved in judgment.

3. God Himself Visited the City. "Then the LORD said, 'The outcry against Sodom and Gomorrah is so great and their sin so grievous that *I will go down and see.*'" (Genesis 18:20, 21, *italics added*).

These three points show us God's standard operating procedure for judgment.

God's Judgment Was an Act of Mercy

In wiping out the entire city of Sodom, God was being merciful to future generations in that city. He spared all future generations of Sodom and Gomorrah the perversion and sin that destroyed their city. From a human point of view, the judgment was severe. However, he only did it after repeatedly extending his grace and mercy to them. He did it to spare future generations the tragedy and sorrow of wickedness. So how can God do it! He does it because he is just. He is merciful. He acts within his justice in the judgment of sin.

If God Is Sovereign, Why Pray?

There are three ways to answer this question. First, you may explain it away, by concluding, "God is not sovereign. He is really not in control. He responds to our prayers. If we pray, he'll answer. If we don't pray, he won't answer." But this option makes *me* sovereign, not God. It puts God up in heaven, wringing his hands, saying, "I'd really like to do such and such, but unless Ed Dobson prays and asks me to, I won't do it." So I become sovereign, and God becomes less than sovereign.

Second, you may decide, "God is sovereign. God is in control. God is at work. Prayer is *not* asking God to *do* something. Rather, prayer is the vehicle through which God merges my desires with his desires." Now it's certainly true that there is a significant point to that principle. Prayer transforms my desires and merges them with the desires of God. But if you study the passages on prayer ("ask and it will be given to you; seek, and you will find, knock and it will be opened to you"), they imply that God responds to our prayers. But if he is sovereign, does it really matter whether or not I pray?

"They forgot the God who saved them, who had done great things in Egypt, miracles in the land of Ham and awesome deeds by the Red Sea. So he said he would destroy them" (Psalm 106:21). God says to the children in Israel, "I have determined to destroy you." Now would that be the will of God? Yes! God says, "This is what I'm going to do. This is my will. This is what I have decided." Now if it was the will of God to destroy the children, then prayer simply would be an acknowledgment of the fact that God was going to do his will. But notice what Moses did: "Had not Moses, his chosen one, stood in the breach [in a similar way to Abraham] before him to keep his wrath from destroying them" (Psalm 106:23).

If God is sovereign, why pray? The answer is that God in his sovereign relationship with human beings has chosen to respond to our intercessions and our prayers, and he delights in responding in prayer. I understand what the sovereignty of God is. I also understand in the life of Abraham and in the life of Moses and through the promises of Jesus Christ that the sovereign God of the universe has chosen within his sovereign will to respond to the prayers and the intercessions of his people. Prayer makes a difference!

Prayer

God, you are God. That means that I do not fully understand your will and ways. Yet I know I can trust you. Even when Abraham and Sarah laughed, you met their need. I yield my life to you. I trust you even when it does not make sense.

Chapter Ten

Sin Will Mess Up Your Life

Sin is a reality of the world in which we live. Enduring the consequences of sin is also a reality of our world. The law of sowing and reaping is an unalterable law of God: "Anyone who receives instruction in the word must share all good things with his instructor. Do not be deceived: God cannot be mocked. A man reaps what he sows" (Galatians 6:7, 8).

In Genesis 19 and 20 we have the story of two people and the consequences of their sinful choices. First, we see Lot and the story of God's judgment on Sodom and Gomorrah. Second, we see the personal consequences of Abraham's dishonesty. While the stories are radically different, the underlying message is the same—you cannot sin and get by with it.

The City Council of Sodom

The two angels arrived at Sodom in the evening, and Lot was sitting in the gateway of the city. When he saw them, he got up to meet them and bowed down with his face to the ground. "My lords," he said, "please turn aside to your servant's house. You can wash your feet and spend the night and then go on your way early in the morning."

"No," they answered, "we will spend the night in the square."

But he insisted so strongly that they did go with him and entered his house. He prepared a meal for them, baking bread without yeast, and they ate. Before they had gone to bed, all the

men from every part of the city of Sodom—both young and old—
surrounded the house.

Genesis 19:1–4

Ancient cities were much different from modern cities. Most
ancient cities had a wall around them and a single entrance. The
entrance was usually an arched gateway between ten and thirty
feet wide. Along each side of the archway was a row of seats.
The political and civil leaders of the city would sit in the gate.
Here they conducted the business of the city. So if you arrived in
a city, as these angels did, and entered in the archway, you would
pass by all the political and civil leaders of the city. Just past the
entrance there was an open marketplace where much of the com-
merce was conducted. Lot is sitting in the gate—he is one of those
leaders. He greets these three visitors and invites them to spend
the night with him. They initially decline the invitation, prefer-
ring to sleep in the open market.

Sin Does Not Make Sense

But he insisted so strongly that they did go with him and
entered his house. He prepared a meal for them, baking bread
without yeast, and they ate. Before they had gone to bed, all the
men from every part of the city of Sodom—both young and old—
surrounded the house. They called to Lot, "Where are the men
who came to you tonight? Bring them out to us so that we can
have sex with them."

Lot went outside to meet them and shut the door behind him
and said, "No, my friends. Don't do this wicked thing. Look, I
have two daughters who have never slept with a man. Let me bring
them out to you, and you can do what you like with them. But
don't do anything to these men, for they have come under the protection of my roof."

Genesis 19:3–8

Some have suggested that God destroyed Sodom because they were not kind to strangers. A clear and simple reading of the text states otherwise. The crowd called to Lot, "Where are the men who came to you tonight? Bring them out to us so that we can have sex with them." This was a city dominated by homosexual sin. The practice of homosexuality is not a biblical expression of human sexuality. In fact, Paul states that such behavior is the result of ignoring God's truth (Romans 1:21–27). While we must be compassionate and understanding to those who genuinely struggle with the temptation to homosexuality, we must not imply that it is a biblical expression of sexuality. Sodom and Gomorrah were destroyed because of their blatant practice of this sin.

Lot tries to appease the crowd. In doing so, he makes an unbelievable statement:

> Look, I have two daughters who have never slept with a man. Let me bring them out to you, and you can do what you like with them. But don't do anything to these men, for they have come under the protection of my roof.
>
> Genesis 19:8

This statement troubles me. I don't have two daughters, I have one. I cannot even fathom what Lot is saying here! He's saying, "Don't do this wicked thing. Here are my daughters. Take them, and whatever you want to do, do it." How could a father even make that kind of statement? It is against reason, against nature, and against love. It is against everything that a father believes. Yet Lot offers his daughters to a sex-crazed mob. He is willing to give them over to gang rape. Shocking!

After looking at all of the commentators, I am still confused. Some suggest that you have to understand ancient eastern hospitality. When you invited people into your house you were obli-

gated by death to protect them. Lot, they say, was simply expressing these customs of hospitality. He was doing whatever was necessary, including the sacrifice of his daughters, for the protection
of these men.

That really doesn't make sense. How could a father make such
an offer?

The only answer I find to be reasonable is that sin does not
make sense. Even though Lot believed in God and tried to live
for him, he had been contaminated by the culture in which he
lived. He did something he thought he would never do, because
sin does not make sense.

We have all had similar experiences. Have you ever said, "Well,
Lord, I want you to forgive me for this sin. I have really struggled in this area of my life. I promise you that I will never do that
again." We have all made similar commitments. Guess what we
did? We walked right out the door and fell into that area of sin
again. It doesn't make sense. It doesn't operate on logical, rational
principles.

If we allow sin to enter into our lives, it will cause us to do
things we thought we would never do, say things we thought we
would never say, and behave in ways that are beyond reason and
beyond logic—just like Lot. Why would a pastor morally default,
when he knows it is wrong and will destroy his life and family?
Why do people jump into bed with strangers, when they know
that AIDS can kill? Why do people abuse alcohol and drugs, when
they know it is destroying them? Why? Why? Why? Because sin
does not make sense. Why did Adam and Eve mess up the whole
human race because of a piece of fruit? Sin does not make sense.
Why did Lot offer his daughters to a bunch of horny men?
Because sin does not make sense.

Sin Will Back You in a Corner

"Get out of our way," they replied. And they said, "This fel-
low came here as an alien, and now he wants to play the judge!
We'll treat you worse than them." They kept bringing pressure
on Lot and moved forward to break down the door.

But the men inside reached out and pulled Lot back into the
house and shut the door. Then they struck the men who were at
the door of the house, young and old, with blindness so that they
could not find the door.

Genesis 19:9–11

Note the disdain that the men of Sodom had for Lot. They
dismissed him as a foreigner. They accused him of being self-
righteous. "Who are *you* to tell *us* what to do? You have lived
in this city. You have participated with us in the business of
Sodom. You know what we're like. And now you have the audac-
ity to judge us? Get out of the way, before we get our hands on
you." Only the intervention of the angels rescued Lot from certain
death.

Judgment—You've Got to Be Kidding!

While the crowd outside the door wanders around in blindness
and bewilderment, the angels declare to Lot the impending judgment of God.

The two men said to Lot, "Do you have anyone else here—
sons-in-law, sons or daughters, or anyone else in the city who
belongs to you? Get them out of here, because we are going to
destroy this place. The outcry to the LORD against its people is so
great that he has sent us to destroy it."

Genesis 19:12, 13

When Lot relates this message of judgment to his family, his future sons-in-law laugh at him.

> So Lot went out and spoke to his sons-in-law, who were pledged to marry his daughters. He said, "Hurry and get out of this place, because the LORD is about to destroy the city!" But his sons-in-law thought he was joking.
>
> Genesis 19:14

"God is going to destroy Sodom?" they ask Lot. "You've got to be kidding. Did you have too much pizza last night. Did you have a nightmare?" Lot's family (including his wife) was so tuned in to the value system of Sodom, they had totally ignored the long-term consequences of their life-style. They lived for the moment—not the future. They were so consumed with pleasure and self-gratification, they forgot about God and the judgment of sin. Jesus alludes to this in the New Testament:

> Just as it was in the days of Noah, so also will it be in the days of the Son of Man. People were eating, drinking, marrying and being given in marriage up to the day Noah entered the ark. Then the flood came and destroyed them all. It was the same in the day of Lot. People were eating and drinking, buying and selling, planting and building.
>
> Luke 17:26–28

There is a significant warning here: Be not deceived, God is not mocked; whatever we sow, we also reap. Sodom was sowing to self, sowing to the flesh, and sowing to pleasure. It was buying and selling, building and planting, marrying and giving in marriage, eating and drinking—with no regard for God. This is the life-style of Western civilization. We have forgotten about our responsibility to God.

Let's Get Out of Here

> With the coming of dawn, the angels urged Lot, saying, "Hurry! Take your wife and your two daughters who are here, or you will be swept away when the city is punished."
>
> When he hesitated, the men grasped his hand and the hands of his wife and of his two daughters and led them safely out of the city, for the LORD was merciful to them.
>
> Genesis 19:15, 16

In spite of the urgency of escaping God's judgment, Lot hesitates. The angels take Lot and his family by the hand and lead them out of Sodom.

When our youngest son, Daniel, was four years old, we were cleaning up the den one night. (It amazes me that no matter how clean you keep the house, a four-year-old can quickly destroy it. It's almost a miracle. In minutes, it's as if a bomb has been dropped in the middle of the house.) It was late in the evening, and I said to Daniel, "Why don't you help us pick up all the Legos?"

Daniel had gladly distributed these hundreds of little building pieces all over the den. How do you think he responded to the suggestion of picking them up? Did he say, "Daddy, I would be delighted. I just love taking them out of the box, and I just love putting them in. Come on, we'll just do it together. This is the most fun I've had all day?" No way! He said, "I can't, I don't have any energy." Four years old! I had to take Daniel's hand and say, "Come on, Daniel, let me show you how."

In this story, Lot is acting like a stubborn four-year-old. As they run for their lives, the angels give Lot and his family three instructions:

1. Don't look back.
2. Don't stop anywhere in the plain.
3. Flee to the mountains.

Given the urgency of these instructions, you would think Lot would obey them with gratitude and enthusiasm. Not so! In fact, he begins to negotiate the demands.

> But Lot said to them, "No, my lords, please! Your servant has found favor in your eyes, and you have shown great kindness to me in sparing my life. But I can't flee to the mountains; this disaster will overtake me, and I'll die. Look, here is a town near enough to run to, and it is small. Let me flee to it—it is very small, isn't it? Then my life will be spared."
>
> Genesis 19:18–20

God's patience with Lot is exceptional. He even grants this request.

Don't Look Back

> By the time Lot reached Zoar, the sun had risen over the land. Then the LORD rained down burning sulfur on Sodom and Gomorrah—from the LORD out of the heavens. Thus he overthrew those cities and the entire plain, including all those living in the cities—and also the vegetation in the land. But Lot's wife looked back, and she became a pillar of salt.
>
> Genesis 19:23–26

The judgment described in these verses is probably a combination of an earthquake and a volcano. "But Lot's wife looked back." This was one of the taboos (v. 17). She was overcome with molten lava and frozen in time. Why? Because she disobeyed the clear instructions of God.

Jesus uses Lot's wife as an illustration in his teaching.

> It was the same in the days of Lot. People were eating and drinking, buying and selling, planting and building. But the day

Lot left Sodom, fire and sulfur rained down from heaven and destroyed them all.

It will be just like this on the day the Son of Man is revealed. On that day no one who is on the roof of his house, with his goods inside, should go down to get them. Likewise, no one in the field should go back for anything. Remember Lot's wife!

Luke 17:28–32

Jesus is describing the characteristics of the last days before he returns. They will be similar to the days of Lot. Then Christ will return in glory and judgment. When Christ delivers us, don't look back. Don't look with affection on the pagan world and its values. Although the context of this passage is future, the principle has an application for today. When Jesus delivers you from sin, don't look back to the sin. When I trust Christ as Savior and Lord, he delivers me from the city of sin (Sodom). I must leave that city behind. If I keep looking back, I will destroy my Christian walk and testimony.

Alcohol, Sex, and Devastation

"So when God destroyed the cities of the plain, *he remembered Abraham*, and he brought Lot out of the catastrophe that overthrew the cities where Lot had lived" (Genesis 19:29, *italics added*). In the middle of this story about Lot, God mentions Abraham. One reason God delivered Lot was his relationship with Abraham. God often demonstrates mercy to others because of a righteous influence in the land and because of intercessory prayer.

Lot and his two daughters left Zoar and settled in the mountains, for he was afraid to stay in Zoar. He and his two daughters lived in a cave. One day the older daughter said to the younger, "Our father is old, and there is no man around here to lie with us, as is the custom all over the earth. Let's get our father to drink wine and then lie with him and preserve our family line through our father."

That night they got their father to drink wine, and the older daughter went in and lay with him. He was not aware of it when she lay down or when she got up.

The next day the older daughter said to the younger, "Last night I lay with my father. Let's get him to drink wine again tonight, and you go in and lie with him so we can preserve our family line through our father."

Genesis 19:30–34

In the earlier part of this story, Lot did the unthinkable with his daughters: He offered them to a sex-starved crowd of men for gang rape. Unthinkable and disgusting. Now these same daughters do the unthinkable with their father. They get him drunk and have sex with him. The offspring of these incestuous acts become the heads of the Moabites and Ammonites. Later in history, these descendants of Lot's daughters would be the bitter enemies of Abraham's descendants (Deuteronomy 2:9, 19; 1 Samuel 14:47; 2 Chronicles 20:1).

History Repeats Itself

When you come to the end of the story of Lot, you are over-whelmed by the devastating consequences of sin. His life is such a contrast to Abraham's—at least in part. In Genesis 20 we read the story of Abraham's failure.

Now Abraham moved on from there into the region of the Negev and lived between Kadesh and Shur. For a while he stayed in Gerar, and there Abraham said of his wife Sarah, "She is my sister." Then Abimelech king of Garar sent for Sarah and took her.

Genesis 20:1, 2

This scenario had occurred twenty-four years earlier. Abraham had gone down into Egypt and lied about his wife in order to protect himself. Read the earlier account carefully.

> Now there was a famine in the land, and Abram went down to Egypt to live there for a while because the famine was severe. As he was about to enter Egypt, he said to his wife Sarai, "I know what a beautiful woman you are. When the Egyptians see you, they will say, 'This is his wife.' Then they will kill me but will let you live. Say you are my sister, so that I will be treated well for your sake and my life will be spared because of you."
>
> Genesis 12:10–13

God intervened in Abraham's life and delivered him from Egypt. Now history repeats itself. What did Abraham learn in Egypt? Whatever it was, he quickly forgot. At this point Sarah is ninety years old. At ninety years old Abimelech notices her beauty. In other words, you could title this chapter, "Life Begins at Ninety." Abimelech takes Sarah into his harem.

You're Dead

"But God came to Abimelech in a dream one night and said to him, 'You are as good as dead because of the woman you have taken; she is a married woman'" (Genesis 20:3). God appears to Abimelech and says, "You are a dead man." Now that will get your attention. God also gives the reason, "Because of the woman you have taken; she is a married woman."

God's warning about death seems a little severe. However, later in the history of Israel, God would give his people clear instructions about his will. We call these instructions the Ten Commandments. One of the commands deals with immorality: "You shall not commit adultery." God also gave a penalty for violating that command, and the penalty was *death*. God's view of sexual purity is so high that he attaches the most severe penalty for its violation.

> Now Abimelech had not gone near her, so he said, "Lord, will you destroy an innocent nation? Did he not say to me, 'She is my sister,' and didn't she also say, 'He is my brother'? I have done this with a clear conscience and clean hands."
> Then God said to him in the dream, "Yes, I know you did this with a clear conscience, and so I have kept you from sinning against me. That is why I did not let you touch her. Now return the man's wife, for he is a prophet, and he will pray for you and you will live. But if you do not return her, you may be sure that you and all yours will die."
>
> Genesis 20:4–7

Abimelech responds, "Lord, how can you kill me? I didn't even touch her." God appreciates Abimelech's objection and reminds the king that he (God) had kept him (Abimelech) from sinning. Notice the language of God. "I have kept you from sinning against *me*" (v. 6, *italics added*). While sin may affect ourselves and others, it is ultimately an act of disobedience against God.

At this point in the story, God has Abimelech's undivided attention. God declares that in addition to judging the king, he will also judge his entire family. The narrative continues, "Early the next morning . . ." (v. 8). If God told me to do something and told me that if I didn't he would kill me and my family, I'd do it as soon as possible.

Why Do People Sin?

> Early the next morning Abimelech summoned all his officials, and when he told them all that had happened, they were very much

afraid. Then Abimelech called Abraham in and said, "What have you done to us? How have I wronged you that you have brought such great guilt upon me and my kingdom? You have done things to me that should not be done." And Abimelech asked Abraham, "What was your reason for doing this?"

Genesis 20:8–10

Abimelech is both afraid and angry. He is afraid of being killed by God. He is mad at Abraham for lying to him about the true identity of Sarah. Abimelech the pagan delivers a sermon to Abraham the prophet. The sermon concludes with the million-dollar question: "What was your reason for doing this?" It's the age-old question "Why?"

As a parent I have frequently asked the same question in many different forms. "Why?" "What was your reason for doing this?" "What was going through your brain?" This is precisely what Abimelech asks Abraham. "What was going through your mind? You sinned against me. You sinned against my kingdom. God nearly killed me. *Why?*" Abraham gives three reasons for his deceptive behavior.

1. Your People Don't Fear God. "Abraham replied, 'I said to myself, "There is surely no fear of God in this place, and they will kill me because of my wife"'" (Genesis 20:11). Abraham says, "I looked around, and I concluded your people don't fear God. Therefore, I lied." The truth was that Abraham was the one who didn't fear God. When Abraham looked around, he was more afraid of Abimelech and his kingdom than he was of God. If Abraham had truly feared the Lord, he would have obeyed and trusted him. The paradox is what he saw as absent in Abimelech was the *very* thing that Abraham lacked—the fear of God.

2. I Didn't Really Lie. "Besides, she really is my sister, the daughter of my father though not of my mother; and she became my wife" (Genesis 20:12). Abraham claims that he did not totally lie. There was some truth in what he said. Therefore he excuses his deception as only a half-truth or a half-lie.

3. It's Really God's Fault. "And when God had me wander from my father's household, I said to her, 'This is how you can show your love to me: Everywhere we go, say of me, "He is my brother."'" (Genesis 20:13). Abraham says, "God had me wander." The implication is that if God had not told him to leave his father's house, he would not have ended up in Abimelech's kingdom. If he had never arrived in Abimelech's kingdom, he would not have lied. "Therefore, it's not my fault, it's really God's fault."

Abimelech responds to Abraham by presenting him offerings to cover the offense. Abraham then prays to God for physical healing and the restoration of childbearing for Abimelech's family.

Learning from Failure

What can we learn from this repeated failure of Abraham? Let me suggest three important lessons.

1. We Can Pass Our Character Flaws to Our Children. We have observed that on two occasions Abraham lied about his wife in order to protect his own life. These events happened before his son Isaac was born. Yet the Scriptures record that the adult Isaac did exactly the same thing.

> Now there was a famine in the land—besides the earlier famine of Abraham's time—and Isaac went to Abimelech king of the Philistines in Gerar. The LORD appeared to Isaac and said, "Do not go down to Egypt; live in the land where I tell you to live. Stay in this land for a while, and I will be with you and will bless you. For to you and your descendants I will give all these lands and will confirm the oath I swore to your father Abraham."

> When the men of that place asked him about his wife, he said, "She is my sister," because he was afraid to say, "She is my wife." He thought, "The men of this place might kill me on account of Rebekah, because she is beautiful."
>
> Genesis 26:1–3, 7

Abraham's dishonesty is repeated in the life of his son. Thank God, this cycle can be broken with the grace and help of God. But in this failure of Abraham, we are reminded of the terrible danger of passing our flaws on to our children.

2. *Honesty Is Not the Best Policy: It's the Only Policy.* Dishonesty *cannot* be defended on circumstances of half-truths. As Christians we are to be a people of truth and honesty.

> You were taught, with regard to our former way of life, to put off your old self, which is being corrupted by its deceitful desires; . . . Therefore each of you must put off falsehood and speak truthfully to his neighbor, for we are all members of one body.
>
> Ephesians 4:22, 25

3. *It Is Better to Fear God Than to Fear Human Beings.* Abraham should have known better than to fear a human being. God had already made promises to Abraham that included the concept of fear: "After this, the word of the LORD came to Abram in a vision: 'Don't be afraid, Abram. I am your shield, your very great reward'" (Genesis 15:1).

God had told Abraham not to fear. Why? Because God would protect him. Abraham forgot that promise when he and Sarah visited the kingdom of Abimelech. One of the bottom-line issues of life is whom or what we fear. If I fear God, then I will trust him, whatever the circumstances. If I fear the circumstances, then I will not trust God in spite of what he has said in his Word. Meditate on the following verses.

Who, then, is the man that fears the LORD? He will instruct him in the way chosen for him. He will spend his days in prosperity, and his descendants will inherit the land.

Psalm 25:12, 13

The LORD is my light and my salvation—whom shall I fear? The LORD is the stronghold of my life—of whom shall I be afraid? When evil men advance against me to devour my flesh, when my enemies and my foes attack me, they will stumble and fall. Though an army besiege me, my heart will not fear; though war break out against me, even then will I be confident.

Psalm 27:1–3

For in the day of trouble he will keep me safe in his dwelling; he will hide me in the shelter of his tabernacle and set me high upon a rock.

Psalm 27:5

I am still confident of this: I will see the goodness of the LORD in the land of the living. Wait for the LORD; be strong and take heart and wait for the LORD.

Psalm 27:13, 14

Prayer

Father, because we are so much like Abraham and Lot, we struggle to fear you and trust you. We find ourselves surrounded by a society that is no friend to grace. We find ourselves struggling to conform and to fit. We find ourselves dishonest, doing and saying things we should never do and say. I pray that we would respect you and trust you, whatever the circumstances. Thank you for being our shield and protection. Lead us not into temptation. Teach us these principles in our everyday life. Deliver us from those besetting sins that so easily defeat us. For we ask it in Jesus' name and for his glory alone. Amen.

Chapter Eleven

God Comes Through— at Last

As I sit writing this chapter, our Christmas decorations surround me. Over the next few days we will gradually put them up. Then our kids will wait for Christmas—and what a wait it will be! Do you remember the week before Christmas, when you were a kid? It was the longest seven days of the year. The presents were wrapped and put under the tree, but you could not open them until Christmas Day. That wait was pure agony. Then there was Christmas Eve—the longest night of the year. Waiting to get what you want is not fun!

Think of how Abraham must have felt about waiting. When Abraham was seventy-five years old, God told him, "I'm going to give you a country. I'm going to make your descendants a great nation." God promised Abraham a son. Now if you were Abraham and Sarah in your sixties and seventies, and God made that promise, you would at least think God would know that the sooner he fulfilled the promise, the better it would be on everybody involved! Do you know how long God waited to fulfill the promise? Twenty-five years! You talk about good news and bad news. At seventy-five years of age, the good news is, "You're going to have a child." The bad news is, "You have to wait twenty-five years."

God Always Comes Through

"Now the LORD was gracious to Sarah as he had said, and the LORD did for Sarah what he had promised. Sarah became pregnant and bore a son to Abraham in his old age, at the very time God had promised him" (Genesis 21:1, 2). After twenty-five years, the miracle happens. God finally comes through. The record of this incredible event seems so brief and factual. Yet we learn much about God in these introductory verses to chapter 21.

You Can Trust God's Word

"Now the LORD was gracious to Sarah as he had *said*, and the LORD did for Sarah what he had *promised*" (*italics added*). God said. God promised. God did. He followed through on his word, and he fulfilled his promise. Granted, it took twenty-five years. Granted, it was a roller-coaster ride of faith and doubt. Granted, Abraham and Sarah messed up along the way. But it *did* happen. God kept his word. This offers encouragement for our own pilgrimage of faith. God may delay (according to our time schedule), but he always keeps his word and his promise.

You Can Trust God's Power

"The LORD *did* for Sarah what he had promised" (*italics added*). God did the impossible. He defied nature and biology. He intervened in the bodies of Abraham and Sarah and performed a miracle. When it comes to living the life of faith, you can trust both God's word and God's power.

Paul expressed his confidence in God's power in the New Testament: "I can do everything through him who gives me strength" (Philippians 4:13).

You Can Trust the Timing of God

"Sarah became pregnant and bore a son to Abraham in his old age, *at the very time* God had promised him" (*italics added*). God is never late.

I know some people who are never on time. Getting somewhere on time is an impossibility for them. Not so with God. The text tells us that with Abraham and Sarah he did what he promised, not a year early or a year late, not a day early or a day late, but on time. In the plan and sovereignty of God, he brought about what he had promised *at the very time*! He made it happen. God's timing may be personally inconvenient for us. God's timing may not make sense. But it is always "at the very time."

Lessons in Trust

Remember, you can trust God's word, power, and timing. In the light of these critical facts, let me suggest three very practical applications.

1. There Are No Obstacles with God. God overruled the biological cycle of Sarah's body, and she became pregnant. Age was not an obstacle to God. In our own lives we constantly come up against obstacles. There are roadblocks to overcome, mountains to climb, and rivers to cross. But with God there are *no* obstacles.

2. There Are No Delays with God. In the lives of Abraham and Sarah, God was neither early nor late. He was right on time. *Delay* is a word to describe our human perspective on life. It is not God's perspective, because with him, there are no delays.

3. There Are No Accidents with God. If God keeps his word and has the power to overcome obstacles and does his work on time, then he is in control. If God is in control, then the events of our lives do not occur by accident. God is never caught by surprise when things happen to us. He is in control (Romans 8:28, 29).

Life Is a Joke

> Abraham gave the name Isaac to the son Sarah bore him. When his son Isaac was eight days old, Abraham circumcised him, as God commanded him. Abraham was a hundred years old when his son Isaac was born to him.
>
> Sarah said, "God has brought me laughter, and everyone who hears about this will laugh with me." And she added, "Who would have said to Abraham that Sarah would nurse children? Yet I have borne him a son in his old age."
>
> Genesis 21:3–7

Abraham names his son *Isaac*, which means "laughter." Both Abraham and Sarah had laughed at God and his promise of a son in their old age. Now the miracle happens, and the promised son is called "laughter."

Sarah, the delighted mother, says, "God has brought me laughter, and everyone who hears about this will laugh with me." This is not the best translation of the Hebrew text. It would be better translated, "And everyone who hears about this will laugh *at* me."

Have you ever met a couple who had several married children and a five-year-old? I have, and when I meet them, I smile inside (really I laugh). They have reared an entire family, and then along comes their "blessing." This is what Sarah is saying: "When people find out that I'm the mother of Isaac and not the grandmother or great-grandmother, they will laugh at me." How true.

Pain Often Accompanies Joy

Isaac grows, and Abraham decides to have a great feast to celebrate. But all is not well. As is often the case in life, pain and joy coexist.

> But Sarah saw that the son whom Hagar the Egyptian had borne
> to Abraham was mocking, and she said to Abraham, "Get rid of
> that slave woman and her son, for that slave woman's son will
> never share in the inheritance with my son Isaac."
>
> Genesis 21:9, 10

There is a play on words in the Hebrew text. It says that Ishmael was "mocking." This verb is the root word for *Isaac*, "laughter." The difference is that the verb is more intense than the name.
It means "cynicism, demeaning laughter, and mockery."

Think of the contrast. God brings Isaac into the lives of Abraham and Sarah. They have laughter. Everyone who sees laughs
as well. Ishmael, Isaac's half-brother, laughs, but it is the laughter
of mockery.

Sarah demands that Abraham get rid of Ishmael and his mother,
Hagar. Ishmael was just as much the son of Abraham as Isaac.
Abraham felt greatly distressed at the thought of sending his son
away, but he did it because Sarah told him to do it.

How Quickly We Forget

> Early the next morning Abraham took some food and a skin
> of water and gave them to Hagar. He set them on her shoulders
> and then sent her off with the boy. She went on her way and wan-
> dered in the desert of Beersheba.
>
> When the water in the skin was gone, she put the boy under
> one of the bushes. Then she went off and sat down nearby, about
> a bowshot away, for she thought, "I cannot watch the boy die."
> And as she sat there nearby, she began to sob.
>
> Genesis 21:14–16

I cannot read these verses without being deeply moved. A son
has been rejected by his father. A mother and son are all alone in
the desert. They are out of water. They are in a state of exhaustion.

There is no one to help. Hagar puts her son under the bush and sits down to watch him die. She begins to sob. No hope. No water. No help. Inevitable death.

But wait a minute! Don't feel too sorry for Hagar. Of all people, she should have known better than to give up. She had been through this once before. When she was pregnant with Ishmael, Sarah became angry and had her thrown out. She wandered in the desert. She was all alone and in despair. But God intervened:

> The angel of the LORD found Hagar near a spring in the desert; it was the spring that is beside the road to Shur.
>
> Then the angel of the LORD told her, "Go back to your mistress and submit to her." The angel added, "I will so increase your descendants that they will be too numerous to count."
>
> The angel of the LORD also said to her: "You are now with child and you will have a son. You shall name him Ishmael, for the LORD has heard of your misery."
>
> Genesis 16:7, 9–11

In fact Hagar named this place *Beer Lahai Roi*, which means "I have seen the one who sees me." The name *Ishmael* means "God hears."

Again Hagar faces desperate circumstances, and again God intervenes.

> God heard the boy crying, and the angel of God called to Hagar from heaven and said to her, "What is the matter, Hagar? Do not be afraid; God has heard the boy crying as he lies there. Lift the boy up and take him by the hand, for I will make him into a great nation."
>
> Then God opened her eyes and she saw a well of water. So she went and filled the skin with water and gave the boy a drink.
>
> Genesis 21:17–19

Notice the focus of what God did. God *heard* and God *called* and God *said* and God *opened* Hagar's eyes. When you have come to the end of your own resources, and you sit down to sob, remember God has a lot of options left—he hears, he calls, he says, and he opens. In fact, there are several things from this story that we need to know in our own desert experiences.

1. God Hears Our Cry. When we are in desperate circumstances, we often wonder if God hears us when we pray. He does. He did for Hagar, and he will for us.

2. God Opens Our Eyes. Hagar was looking down. She was watching her son. She was sobbing. She was out of touch with the world around her. Only her life and her son's life mattered at the moment. But God opened her eyes to see beyond the narrow vision of her pain. When she looked, she saw a well of water.

3. God Is with Us. "God was with the boy as he grew up. He lived in the desert and became an archer. While he was living in the Desert of Paran, his mother got a wife for him from Egypt" (Genesis 21:20, 21).

"God was with the boy." What a statement. When you go through the desert, remember God is with you. David says, "Even though I walk through the valley of the shadow of death, I will fear no evil, for you are with me" (Psalm 23:4).

It's Hard to Watch Your Kids Wander

One sentence strikes me in this chapter: "The matter distressed Abraham greatly because it concerned his son" (Genesis 21:11). Some of you have watched a son or a daughter make wrong decisions and choices. That child moved in destructive directions. Your sons and daughters walked away from God. You watched them go out into the desert, and you so desperately wanted to stop them. You knew there was nothing you could do. Your heart was broken—like the heart of Abraham.

May I remind you of three things:

1. *God hears your cry.* He is not deaf. He is not ignoring you.
2. *God can open a way in the life of your wayward children when they sit there in the desert.* God can open a way.
3. Here's what I really want you to grasp. Even though Ishmael was outside the covenant relationship (he was not the covenant son), it says, *"God was with the boy."*

If I could say one word of encouragement to you, it would be this: You never wander beyond the care of a sovereign God who keeps his word. Wherever your son or daughter is, God is there, and he can open a way.

Prayer

God, thank you for your promises. Thank you that you keep your promises. Help us to trust you in the face of obstacles, in spite of delays, and when it appears that there is no hope. Remind us that with you there is always hope.

Chapter Twelve

Passing God's Exam

Final Exams. The words still conjure up nightmares for me: burning the midnight oil to memorize volumes of facts; noticing my increased heart rate as the teacher passed out the test; staring into space and trying to remember a name or a date. We have all been through the stress.

I remember when I came to the end of my course work in doctoral studies at the University of Virginia. Before you start into your dissertation, you have to take written and oral exams. Now oral exams have never bothered me! But written exams are a different story. I'm not great when it comes to writing! I took three months to prepare for my written exams. I buried myself in the books every spare moment. Every evening I gave up television, exercise, and relaxation. For several months I read and studied, read and studied. I put information on cassette tapes and played them in my car. I wrote information on three-by-five cards and carried them everywhere. I knew that if I failed the written exams, I was out of the program. That will get your attention!

Finally the day came when I drove to the university to spend several days taking the exams. I knew there would be five written questions. It all seemed so unfair. All that work, all those books, and all that effort were reduced to five questions in a sealed envelope. One of the questions dealt with research and methodology, another with administration, another with the history of higher education, another with management in a university setting. And the last question, which I feared the most, dealt with business administration.

I remember going to the law library at the University of Virginia. I prayed before I started and said, "Lord, help me out!" I opened up the envelope and for several days answered those five questions. I'm glad it is over (by the way, I passed and finished my degree), and I will always remember the stress.

Abraham has been walking with God for many years. Things are now going well. He has a son, and the future looks good for the first time in years. But he is about to take his final exam—and it's a tough one.

Abraham Had Failed Before

"Some time later God tested Abraham. He said to him, 'Abraham!' 'Here I am,' he replied" (Genesis 22:1).

Success breeds success. If you do well throughout the semester, chances are pretty good that you will do well on the final exam. The problem with Abraham is that he has been tested before—and failed. He does not have a good record coming into this final exam. God had previously tested him on at least three occasions.

1. God Had Tested His Obedience. Shortly after God had called Abraham to leave his country and extended family, Abraham had encountered a famine. He did not know what to do. Instead of listening to God and following him, Abraham decided to solve his own problem by going down to Egypt to get food. He failed to obey God and in the process made a mess of his life (Genesis 12).

2. God Had Tested His Faith. Most of the time that Abraham followed God, God was testing his faith. When God first called Abraham, God promised to make his descendants great. The first step in accomplishing that purpose was to give Abraham a son, and God promised to do just that. While God delayed, Abraham became impatient. Failing to trust God, Abraham decided, with the advice of Sarah, to help God by having a son through Hagar. Ishmael was born. He was the son of Abraham's failure—not his faith. Abraham failed the test of faith and again made a mess out of his life.

3. God Had Tested His Fear of God. When Abraham went down into the country of Abimelech, he lied about his wife Sarah. Abimelech took Sarah into his harem (assuming she was Abraham's sister, as Abraham had told him). God spoke to Abimelech and threatened to kill him and his family if he did not give Sarah back to Abraham. Abimelech asked Abraham why he lied. Abraham gave a weak excuse: "I thought there was no fear of God in this place." The truth of the matter was that *Abraham* did not fear God. He was more afraid of Abimelech than he was of God. By failing the test of fearing God, he made a mess of his life.

Abraham had failed to obey God, trust God, and fear God. The result—he made a mess. Now God comes to Abraham to test him again in these same areas. "Will you obey me, Abraham? Will you trust me, Abraham? Will you fear me, Abraham?" And the test is the most overwhelming choice Abraham has *ever* had to make.

The Test of Obedience

Some time later God tested Abraham. He said to him, "Abraham!"

"Here I am," he replied.

Then God said, "Take your son, your only son, Isaac, whom you love, and go to the region of Moriah. Sacrifice him there as a burnt offering on one of the mountains I will tell you about."

Genesis 22:1, 2

Before we examine the test of obedience, we must ponder the troubling ethical nature of God's request. Why would God order a human sacrifice? This seems pagan and antithetical to the character of God.

Following the Pagan Tradition. Some commentators suggest that Abraham was adopting the pagan religious practice of his day. Human sacrifice was common in the country where Abraham lived. The development of Jewish religion began with pagan sacrifices, these commentators theorize, and then became more sophisticated in later years. This is the liberal interpretation.

The problem, however, with this perspective is that God ordered the sacrifice.

A Spiritual Test. Others have suggested that God was only testing Abraham's spirit. It was, they claim, a test of attitude—not the request for a literal sacrifice.

The problem with this perspective is that the narrative clearly implies that Abraham had a literal sacrifice in mind. There were wood, a knife, fire, and an altar. God alone had the right to demand life. He was the one who gave life (Isaac), and he was the one who could ask it in return.

A Prophetic Vision. The narrative and the strange request have prophetic implications. I believe this is why God made this startling demand. On the same mountain, hundreds of years later, another Father would offer his Son as a sacrifice. Only this time there would be no substitute. This is the piece of land where Jesus would die on the cross.

The shocking nature of God's request to Abraham is a reminder of the terrible price that Jesus paid to purchase our redemption. It cost him his life.

Early the next morning Abraham got up and saddled his donkey. He took with him two of his servants and his son Isaac. When he had cut enough wood for the burnt offering, he set out for the

place God had told him about. On the third day Abraham looked
up and saw the place in the distance.

Genesis 22:3, 4

Now back to the test of obedience. Abraham's response to God
was immediate, "Early the next morning." He did not second-
guess God. He did not argue, as he had when God was about to
destroy Sodom. He didn't offer other alternatives. He obeyed.

Put yourself in the place of Abraham. He waited for twenty-
five years for the promised son. Isaac is now sixteen to twenty
years of age. Everything is going well, and then God makes a
strikingly difficult request. "Take the son you waited for, the son
whom I promised you, and make a fifty-mile journey. Offer him as
a sacrifice." For three long, agonizing, perplexing days, Abraham
makes the journey.

I wonder what was going through his mind during these three
days. I am confident his whole life played before him over and
over again. He thought of the long pilgrimage of faith. He thought
about his failures. Maybe God was punishing him for disobedience. He thought about his son—Isaac. Laughter. Now there was
nothing to laugh about. His entire world was about to come crash-
ing down. He was about to lose the only thing that mattered—
his son. *Why couldn't God take me and not him?* Yet whatever
he thought, he kept walking. Unknown to him, he was passing
the test of obedience.

The Test of Faith

"He said to his servants, 'Stay here with the donkey while I
and the boy go over there. We will worship and then we will come
back to you'" (Genesis 22:5). Abraham made an incredible statement that reflected mature faith in God. He said to the servants,
"We [father and son] are going over there to worship, and we

[father and son] *will come back to you.*" Abraham knew what God wanted him to do—sacrifice his son. But Abraham has such faith in God that he knew that somehow Isaac would be brought to life, and they would return together.

How could Abraham be so sure? His faith was connected to the promise of God, the power of God, and the provision of God.

1. Abraham Trusted the Promise of God. "But God said to him, 'Do not be so distressed about the boy and your maidservant. Listen to whatever Sarah tells you, because it is through Isaac that your offspring will be reckoned'" (Genesis 21:12).

In the last chapter, God had promised that Isaac was the son through which future generations would come. Even though the sacrifice of Isaac seemed to contradict that, Abraham did not lose his confidence in the promise. The present reality would not alter the reality of God's promise. Isaac was the son of promise and would remain so. Therefore Abraham could say, "We're going up, and we're coming back down."

2. Abraham Trusted the Power of God. One of the beautiful things about the New Testament is that it often gives us additional insight into Old Testament stories. This is true in the story we are now studying.

> By faith Abraham, when God tested him, offered Isaac as a sacrifice. He who had received the promises was about to sacrifice his one and only son, even though God had said to him, "It is through Isaac that your offspring will be reckoned." Abraham reasoned that God could raise the dead, and figuratively speaking, he did receive Isaac back from death.
>
> Hebrews 11:17–19

"Abraham reasoned that God could raise the dead." He was confident of God's power. He figured, *I'll go up this mountain; I'll put the wood on the altar; I'll sacrifice my son. We'll both*

*come back down, because I know God has the power to raise the
dead.*

3. Abraham Trusted the Provision of God. The story continues:

> Abraham took the wood for the burnt offering and placed it on
> his son Isaac, and he himself carried the fire and the knife. As the
> two of them went on together, Isaac spoke up and said to his father
> Abraham, "Father?"
> "Yes, my son?" Abraham replied.
> "The fire and wood are here," Isaac said, "but where is the
> lamb for the burnt offering?"
> Abraham answered, "God himself will provide the lamb for
> the burnt offering, my son." And the two of them went on together.
>
> Genesis 22:6–8

Isaac is pretty observant. "Dad," he says. "We've got everything we need for a sacrifice except the lamb." Like a dagger, this
question must have pierced the heart of Abraham. Perhaps for a
brief moment, pain seized his soul. But his answer demonstrates a
further dimension of his faith. "God will provide the lamb," Abraham responds.

Father and son walked on together. The question of faith had
been raised. The answer had been given, and Abraham had passed
the test. His faith was in the promise of God, in the power of God,
and in the provision of God. He knew God would not fail him
now.

The Test of Fear

> When they reached the place God had told him about, Abra-
> ham built an altar there and arranged the wood on it. He bound
> his son Isaac and laid him on the altar, on top of the wood. Then
> he reached out his hand and took the knife to slay his son.
>
> Genesis 22:9, 10

What does it mean to fear God? It means to reverence him as the sovereign of the universe. It means to trust him implicitly and to obey him without question. This is precisely what Abraham is now compelled to do. He raises the knife to kill his son. His action contradicts every fiber of his being. It defies his nature, his future, and his love. Yet God said, "Do it." In this trembling moment Abraham must choose God over every natural instinct. He must obey when it defies all human logic. He must obey when it forfeits his future. He must obey—whatever the consequences. To take this radical step of obedience, Abraham must fear (reverence) God over everyone and everything else. Moved with fear, he starts this final act of obedience. Before he completes it, God intervenes.

Abraham looked up and there in a thicket he saw a ram caught by its horns. He went over and took the ram and sacrificed it as a burnt offering instead of his son. So Abraham called that place the LORD Will Provide. And to this day it is said, "On the mountain of the LORD it will be provided."

The angel of the LORD called to Abraham from heaven a second time and said, "I swear by myself, declares the LORD, that because you have done this and have not withheld your son, your only son, I will surely bless you and make your descendants as numerous as the stars in the sky and as the sand on the seashore. Your descendants will take possession of the cities of their enemies, and through your offspring all nations on earth will be blessed, because you have obeyed me."

Then Abraham returned to his servants, and they set off together for Beersheba. And Abraham stayed in Beersheba.

Genesis 22:13–19

Some Thoughts About the Nature of Exams

In our own personal pilgrimage of faith, we are constantly tested. These tests usually come in the same three areas as Abraham's: Are we willing to obey God; are we willing to trust God; are we willing to fear God?

Abraham's story also reveals the characteristics of God's tests.

1. When God Tests Us, He Often Touches a Precious Area of Our Lives. God touched the most precious thing that Abraham had—his son. The same is true in our lives. God knows how to get our attention.

2. The Test Is Often Lonely. Abraham and Isaac went together. It was a lonely experience. The rest of the family, the hired men, and servants stayed behind. Often God's test requires us to struggle—alone. It would be nice to have everybody with you. But more often than not, we walk to Mount Moriah by ourselves.

3. The Test Demands Unwavering Faith in God's Word. The bottom line for Abraham was clear. "Will I believe in God's word or not?" The same is true for us. The bottom line is often the same. "Do I really believe God's Word [the Bible] or not?" This is one of the reasons it is important to read, study, and memorize the Bible. When we face comprehensive exams, we will need to know and believe God's Word.

4. Deliverance May Not Come Till the Last Minute. Abraham called God *Jehovah-jireh,* "the Lord provides." He does provide. But as with Abraham, the provision may not come until the last minute.

Prayer

Father, we acknowledge that we do not enjoy the Mount Moriah experience. But we are also quick to acknowledge that until we have climbed that mountain of difficulty we never really know you as the one who is Jehovah-jireh—the God who provides. In the test of life and faith, I pray that we would trust your promise, your power, and your provision. You are *all* we need. May we even embrace your testing, because in our deepest point of need we know you are there and you provide. Encourage those who have heavy burdens. Renew us with a sense of your promise and your power and your provision. For we ask it in Jesus' name and for his glory. Amen.

Chapter Thirteen

Faith in the Face of Death

"Sarah lived to be a hundred and twenty-seven years old. She died at Kiriath Arba (that is, Hebron) in the land of Canaan, and Abraham went to mourn for Sarah and to weep over her" (Genesis 23:1, 2).

In Old Testament culture, when someone passed away, family and friends went into an extensive period of mourning. They would weep and wail and play funeral songs on the flute. Some would put on sackcloth; others would fast and pray or put dust on their heads. This period of intense sorrow was called "the mourning." The length of this mourning time varied. For example, when Jacob died in Egypt, the Egyptians mourned for seventy days. When Aaron and Moses died, the children of Israel set aside thirty days in which they devoted their energies to mourning.

When you get to the New Testament, you see the issues of mourning and grief raised to a new level. During the New Testament era, you could actually hire professional mourners. These people made their living by going to various funerals. They went from village to village, and they were experts in expressing grief. By the time Jesus comes on the scene, the emotions of mourning and grieving had reached unbelievable heights.

In the face of death and mourning there is hope, and the New Testament expresses that hope in the form of a person—Jesus Christ. Jesus Christ makes the difference.

"Brothers, we do not want you to be ignorant about those who fall asleep, or to grieve like the rest of men who have no hope" (1 Thessalonians 4:13). When facing death and the life hereafter, believers weep and mourn the loss of a loved one. But while we grieve and mourn, we face death with a different perspective. We have hope—*HOPE!* As a pastor, I am called upon to meet with families in times of grief and loss. I do not have the language to describe the contrast between an unbelieving family and a believing one in the face of death. There are tears in both cases. There is grief. There is loss. Yes, there is mourning. Both experience emptiness, knowing the void that is left behind cannot be filled by any other human being. But strikingly the believing family has an inner, abiding, sustaining hope. Paul reminds us that if "we believe Jesus died and rose again [and he did] we also believe that those who die will rise again" (*see* 1 Thessalonians 4:14). There is eternity with the Savior and with those who have gone before.

Although Abraham did not have the advantage of New Testament teaching, nevertheless he expressed faith in the face of loss. The man who lived by faith was able to face the death of his wife the same way.

When God Does Something, Others Take Notice

> Then Abraham rose from beside his dead wife and spoke to the Hittites. He said, "I am an alien and a stranger among you. Sell me some property for a burial site here so I can bury my dead."
>
> The Hittites replied to Abraham, "Sir, listen to us. You are a mighty prince among us. Bury your dead in the choicest of our tombs. None of us will refuse you his tomb for burying your dead."
>
> Genesis 23:3–6

Abraham begins negotiations to buy a burial site for Sarah from the Hittites. The Hittites offer Abraham any site he wants, and they call him "a mighty prince among us." Even the pagan peoples around Abraham recognized that he was an unusual person. The underlying principle is this: When God does something supernatural in your life, others will sit up and pay attention!

This is not the first time this recognition was made. "At that time Abimelech and Phicol the commander of his forces said to Abraham, 'God is with you in everything you do'" (Genesis 21:22). Abimelech was a pagan king, not a follower of Abraham's God. Yet he and the commander of his forces recognized that God was with Abraham in a special and unique way.

I am convinced that one of the reasons we make such a little dent in the real world is that God "ain't doin' nothin'" in our lives. We are on autopilot. If God were really doing supernatural things in our lives, transforming us into the image of Christ, it would be so obvious to the people we work with that we would have opportunity after opportunity to share our lives and experiences with them. The world would sit up and pay attention.

There is an old saying that people will drive from all over to see a fire burn. The same is true in regard to our churches and personal lives. If we are allowing God to work in our lives, people will drive from all over to see us on fire for God.

Cross-Cultural Sensitivity

"Then Abraham rose and bowed down before the people of the land, the Hittites" (Genesis 23:7). Abraham continued his negotiations for a burial site. He arose and bowed before the people of the land. This was proper etiquette and was expected. Abraham understood the customs of the Hittites and accommodated them by not offending them with his behavior. This is an important principle in dealing with others.

Later in the Book of Genesis, Joseph appears before Pharaoh and changes his behavior in order not to offend the ruler: "So Pharaoh sent for Joseph, and he was quickly brought from the dungeon. When he had shaved and changed his clothes, he came before Pharaoh" (Genesis 41:14).

Joseph shaved and changed his clothes. Why? Because to appear before Pharaoh unshaven and with prison clothes would have offended the ruler of Egypt. Joseph knew that this would hinder his ability to communicate the Word of God and the interpretation of the dream.

This same principle of cultural adaptation is critical for communicating the gospel. Paul affirms it in the New Testament.

> Though I am free and belong to no man, I make myself a slave to everyone, to win as many as possible. To the Jews I became like a Jew, to win the Jews. To those under the law I became like one under the law (though I myself am not under the law), so as to win those under the law. To those not having the law I became like one not having the law (though I am not free from God's law but am under Christ's law), so as to win those not having the law. To the weak I became weak, to win the weak. I have become all things to all men so that by all possible means I might save some. I do all this for the sake of the gospel, that I may share in its blessings.
>
> 1 Corinthians 9:19–23

Paul is saying, "If I am going to target a certain group of people, I must understand that group—how they think, how they live, and how they behave. I must adapt my life-style and methodology so as not to offend them. I must build a bridge right into their culture and then share the gospel of Christ." If you read the Book of Acts, that's what Paul puts into practice. On one occasion he is quoting Old Testament Law, convincing the Jew that Christ is Messiah. On Mars Hill he does not quote Old Testament Law.

Rather, he reasons from the Greek and ancient philosophers that the unknown God whom they worship is the God who sent Jesus Christ down to this earth. In other words, Paul understood that in order to reach people, you make adjustments in your personal life for the sake of the gospel.

We understand this principle in a missions setting. When you go to another country, you learn the language and culture of those people so you can share Jesus Christ in a culturally sensitive way. But that same principle applies here in the United States. We have a tendency to think that once we've built a beautiful sanctuary, everybody will come and get saved. However, God's strategy is for us as individual believers to infiltrate all of the sectors of this society: to the Jew as a Jew, to the weak as weak; and to those under the Law as those under the Law. So that somehow, some-way, by all possible means, we might win people to the good news of the gospel of Christ.

The message has never changed. It is the good news of the gospel of Jesus Christ. What we learn in the life of Abraham, Joseph, and in the strategy of the apostle Paul, is that the context changes, the culture changes, and the method changes. Paul adapts to all of that so that he can have the privilege of sharing Jesus Christ.

Paying the Price

Ephron the Hittite was sitting among his people and he replied to Abraham in the hearing of all the Hittites who had come to the gate of his city. "No, my lord," he said. "Listen to me; I give you the field, and I give you the cave that is in it. I give it to you in the presence of my people. Bury your dead."

Again Abraham bowed down before the people of the land and he said to Ephron in their hearing, "Listen to me, if you will. I

will pay the price of the field. Accept it from me so I can bury
my dead there."

Ephron answered Abraham, "Listen to me, my lord; the land
is worth four hundred shekels of silver, but what is that between
me and you? Bury your dead."

Abraham agreed to Ephron's terms and weighed out for him
the price he had named in the hearing of the Hittites: four hundred shekels of silver, according to the weight current among the
merchants.

Genesis 23:10–16

Ephron the Hittite offers to give Abraham the field. This is not
a gift in the sense that it cost nothing. He is saying what many
television evangelists say, "Give me a hundred dollars, and I will
give you this free book." He is not really giving you anything.
And this is the understanding here. Ephron said, "I'll give you
this." But he has a price in mind.

Many doubt the historicity of the Book of Genesis. They
believe you can trust the Bible in the area of theology, but it was
never intended to be a book of history. Therefore, when you come
to the historical events, they say you really can't trust the Bible.
For many years scholars called this particular chapter into question. They argued that the transaction of this chapter did not fit
the general practices of ancient culture. Therefore, they questioned the Bible's historicity.

A number of years ago, however, archaeologists discovered
an ancient Hittite settlement and began digging up documents—
specifically, legal land contract documents. They discovered from
these that land negotiations were conducted in precisely the way
described in this chapter. This reminds us that if it looks as if
there is something wrong with the Bible, wait long enough, and
science and archaeology will eventually catch up. You can
absolutely trust the historicity of the Bible.

Before I took my doctoral exams at the University of Virginia, I was asked by the chairman of my committee, "Now suppose we can give you empirical data that absolutely contradict the Bible. What are you going to do?"

He thought he had me in a bind. I sensed that he wanted me to say, "I will trust the research, the validity of all this information achieved through proper scientific process. I will dismiss the Bible." But I answered: "I will accept the validity of the scientific research, and I'll put it over here in my brain. I will also accept the reliability and historicity of the Scripture. I know at this point, the two cannot be reconciled. But somewhere in the future, there will be deeper scientific research, and ultimately they will be reconciled. Because I have absolute faith and confidence that this book is without error—Genesis to Revelation."

All of Life Is Lived by Faith

What do we learn from Sarah's death? We learn that all life is lived by faith. We begin by faith, we live each day by faith; we finish by faith.

We Begin by Faith

Then the word of the LORD came to him: "This man will not be your heir, but a son coming from your own body will be your heir." He took him outside and said, "Look up at the heavens and count the stars—if indeed you can count them." Then he said to him, "So shall your offspring be."

Abram believed the LORD, and he credited it to him as righteousness.

Genesis 15:4–6

This is the conversion experience of Abraham. Abraham believed the Lord. He was saved by faith. God credited his account with righteousness. That's how we get saved. We don't work for it. We don't earn it. We don't get baptized in it. We're not confirmed into it. We are saved by grace, through faith in Jesus Christ (Ephesians 2:8, 9).

We Live Each Day by Faith

Against all hope, Abraham in hope believed and so became the father of many nations, just as it had been said to him, "So shall your offspring be." Without weakening in his faith, he faced the fact that his body was as good as dead—since he was about a hundred years old—and that Sarah's womb was also dead. Yet he did not waver through unbelief regarding the promise of God, but was *strengthened in his faith* and gave glory to God.

Romans 4:18–20, *italics added*

Abraham lived each day by faith. His life of faith was a growing experience. It says that Abraham was strengthened, built up in his faith. Now we have studied his life enough to know that he failed miserably many times. Abraham doubted, disobeyed, and failed to trust God. He ran from God. In spite of these failures, overall he continued to grow in his faith.

We Finish by Faith

By faith Abraham, even though he was past age—and Sarah herself was barren—was enabled to become a father because he considered him faithful who had made the promise. And so from this one man, and he as good as dead, came descendants as numerous as the stars in the sky and as countless as the sand on the seashore. All of these people were still living by faith when they died.

Hebrews 11:11–13

Now notice God had made Abraham two basic promises. "Look up at the stars. That's your offspring. Can you count them?"

"No."

"You won't be able to count your offspring."

Promise number two said, "Look around at the land in every direction. I'm going to give it to you."

Abraham believed God. Abraham comes to the end of his life. Rather than a multitude of stars for offspring, he has one son, who is thirty-seven years old when Sarah dies. Rather than a land, Abraham has one field. He takes Sarah to the promised land and buries her by faith. He has not received the final fulfillment of the promise.

Prayer

Father, remind us again that we are saved by faith. We live each day by faith. We die by faith. Increase our faith in your presence, in your promise, and in the power of the resurrected Jesus Christ. In his name we pray. Amen.

Chapter Fourteen

Finding a Wife Can Be a Tough Job

In *The Birth Order Book* (Revell, 1985), Kevin Leman cites the following ad that appeared in a major metropolitan newspaper:

> Christian, blond, blue eyes, 5'2", 100 pounds, professional female, no dependents, wishes to meet Protestant Christian, professional man in 30's with a college degree who has compassion for animals and people, loves nature, exercise and physical fitness (no team sports), music, church and home life. Desires non-smoker, non-drinker, slender 5'7" to 6', lots of head hair, intelligent, honest, trustworthy, sense of humor, excellent communicator of feelings, very sensitive, gentle, affectionate, giving, encouraging and helpful to others, no temper or ego problems, secure within and financially, health conscious, neat and clean, extremely considerate and dependable. I believe in old-fashioned morals and values. If you do and are interested in a possible Christian commitment, write to the following box. Please include recent color photo and address.

Whoever placed this ad will probably grow old—alone. There are no perfect people.

How do you go about finding a spouse?

I received a letter recently from one of our single missionaries, Carrie Sydnor. Carrie works with the Navigators. She is a journalist and writes about God at work in the Third World. Our church supports her. The letter, dated June 2, 1989, says, "Dear Special Friend, wonder of wonders, miracle of miracles, at the tender age of forty-seven, I'm getting married. Here's how the drama unfolded." And she begins to tell the story of how she met the man she is marrying.

She talks about being heavy hearted in her devotions about her desire for a husband. After reading "the desire of the diligent shall be fully satisfied" (Proverbs 13:4), she prayed again for a husband as she is so diligent that she burnt herself out once.

Then she talks about an aversion to junk mail. "I leave it all for my roommate to read." She goes on. . . . "But she opened and read a piece of mail from a dating service." On a lark she filled out their survey which led to an interview. She was told this dating service had many Christian members (it didn't), so she joined. A few months later, a gentleman named King Coffman also filled out a survey to this dating service on a lark and soon joined. They were brought together and introduced.

Before they were introduced, Carrie had been struck by the fact that Abraham had a God that called things that were not as if they were, thus creating them out of nothing (Romans 4:17). Since it was obvious to her that there was no man for her, she decided to trust God to make one out of nothing. "So, since God would have to create him from scratch, I had given him a list of thirty-three serious and frivolous qualities I wanted God to create in this man. For example, that this man would read the Scriptures with a heart to obey them and that he had no potbelly." She goes on to say that the person she met had thirty-one of the thirty-three qualities. So the wedding date was set for July 23 in Los Angeles.

We are both utterly awed by God's lavish goodness, as we both feel that we got much more than we had ever hoped for in a spouse. Ephesians 5 states that God intended that a man and wife would be a replica of Christ's relationship to the church. Please pray that ours would be a marriage that constantly advertises how sweet it is to walk with Christ.

What a story!

As Abraham comes to the end of his life, he is concerned that his son Isaac find an appropriate bride, to guarantee the future promises of God. The entire twenty-fourth chapter of Genesis is devoted to this exciting and unusual story. From this story we can draw certain biblical principles that are critical in making the choice in regard to a spouse.

A Good Marriage Is Built on a Spiritual Foundation

> Abraham was now old and well advanced in years, and the LORD had blessed him in every way. He said to the chief servant in his household, the one in charge of all that he had, "Put your hand under my thigh. I want you to swear by the LORD, the God of heaven and the God of earth, that you will not get a wife for my son from the daughters of the Canaanites, among whom I am living, but will go to my country and my own relatives and get a wife for my son Isaac."
>
> Genesis 24:1–4

Sarah has been dead for three years, and Isaac has just turned forty when Abraham begins the search for his son's bride.

Because the Canaanites worshiped pagan gods, and Abraham knew Isaac's marrying a pagan would mean his spiritual destruction, the concerned father makes his servant Eliezar swear that he will not seek a bride from among the Canaanites. Abraham instructs Eliezar to travel 450 miles to get a bride from among Abraham's family.

Abraham knew the critical necessity of building a marriage on a common spiritual foundation.

In the New Testament, Paul articulates the same principle:

> Do not be yoked together with unbelievers. For what do righteousness and wickedness have in common? Or what fellowship can light have with darkness? What harmony is there between Christ and Belial? What does a believer have in common with an unbeliever? What agreement is there between the temple of God and idols? For we are the temple of the living God. As God has said: "I will live with them and walk among them, and I will be their God, and they will be my people."
>
> 2 Corinthians 6:14–16

This principle of spiritual conformity extends beyond the marital relationship. It could be a business relationship, a partnership, a marriage, or a dating relationship. Paul says that believers are committed to God's Word; unbelievers are not. They are not operating on the same spiritual principles, and they do not have the same spiritual foundation. Therefore, it is wrong to mix the two together. Their value systems conflict.

As a pastor, I am often asked if I recommend a believer dating (or marrying) a nonbeliever. My answer is always the same. I do *not* recommend it.

Often the other person responds, "Well, I can win him [or her] to the Lord."

Maybe so. Maybe not. I have dealt with many believers who began relationships with nonbelievers with the idea of winning them to Christ. Sometimes they did. Most of the time they did not. I cannot express the frustration level of believers whose spouses show no interest in spiritual matters.

Beyond the issue of salvation, there are other spiritual issues to be considered in building a healthy marital relationship. I divide these issues into three areas:

1. The absolutes.
2. Theological convictions.
3. Preferences.

The ultimate issue, as we have already stated, is commitment to Christ. As a believer, does a prospective mate have a heart to obey God and to live by his Word? I'm not talking about someone who says, "Well, I signed a card, and I made a commitment," but someone for whom Jesus Christ is the center and the focus of life. Those are the absolutes. The bottom line—a believer.

Then there are convictions, which deal with how I interpret the Scriptures: whether I believe in sprinkling or in baptism by immersion, whether I am reformed or dispensational, Methodist or Presbyterian or Baptist. None of these issues determine my eternal destiny. But all are important for those of us who take the Bible seriously.

If your are developing a relationship with a believer, you need to go beyond commitment to Christ and talk through some of your convictions about the Bible. If there is serious disagreement, this could lead to major tension in your relationship.

The third area deals with preferences. Preferences include areas where the Bible does not speak directly, but we nevertheless practice certain traditions. For example, my wife and I agree on the absolutes. We agree on the convictions. One area where we disagree is music style. Lorna is a classically trained pianist. She loves classical music of all kinds. I care little for this style of music. I am a rock-and-roll enthusiast. Lorna can't stand rock and roll—for her it's not even music.

Building a healthy marriage means total agreement on the absolutes, understanding on the convictions, and tolerance on the preferences.

Singleness Is Better than a Wrong Marriage

> The servant asked him, "What if the woman is unwilling to come back with me to this land? Shall I then take your son back to the country you came from?"
>
> "Make sure that you do not take my son back there," Abraham said. "The LORD, the God of heaven, who brought me out of my father's household and my native land and who spoke to me and promised me an oath, saying, 'To your offspring I will give this land'—he will send his angel before you so that you can get a wife for my son from there."
>
> Genesis 24:5–7

Eliezar raises an important question. "If I go all the way there," he says, "and if the bride will not come back, what should I do? Shall I take Isaac back there?" His suggestion is logical. If the woman will not come to Isaac, Isaac should go to the woman.

Abraham emphatically answers, "Don't take Isaac back!" He gives two reasons. First, God brought him from that country. To return would be an act of disobedience. Second, God promised Abraham the land, and his descendants must stay there and claim it. It's better to obey God than give in to our selfish demands. It is more noble to be single than to marry in disobedience to God.

One of the major reasons marriages break up is selfishness, an attitude that exclaims, "I want what I want on my terms, under my conditions. Since I am not getting it out of this relationship, I will leave. I will get out, because what I need and what I want I have got to have."

You know what is more important than our needs—obedience to the Word of God. In our culture everyone is into self—self-promotion, self-actualization, and self-esteem. I understand the importance of all of those things, but the bottom line is, "Am I willing to obey God, even if that obedience costs what I perceive to be my needs?"

Abraham says to Eliezar, "Eliezar, there is something that is more important than Isaac's going back to get the bride, and it is this: We must obey and trust God."

When Seeking a Spouse, Ask for Direction from God

> Then the servant took ten of his master's camels and left, taking with him all kinds of good things from his master. He set out for Aram Naharaim and made his way to the town of Nahor. He had the camels kneel down near the well outside the town; it was toward evening, the time the women go out to draw water.
>
> Then he prayed, "O LORD, God of my master Abraham, give me success today, and show kindness to my master Abraham. See, I am standing beside this spring, and the daughters of the towns-people are coming out to draw water. May it be that when I say to a girl, 'Please let down your jar that I may have a drink,' and she says, 'Drink, and I'll water your camels too'—let her be the one you have chosen for our servant Isaac. By this I will know that you have shown kindness to my master."
>
> Genesis 24:10–14

Eliezar had just made a 450-mile journey. He crossed to the east side of the Jordan River, traveled north on the King's Highway, to Damascus and northeast up the Bika Valley. He crossed deserts in intense heat. Finally he arrives.

The first thing he does is pray: "O LORD, God of my master Abraham, give me success today." The Hebrew text is beautiful at this point; it states, "Let there come to meet me, success." Eliezar gives God some conditions. He wants God to identify Isaac's bride by unusual behavior on her part. He decides to ask the women to give him a drink. The bride will offer him a drink and also offer to water his ten camels (v. 10).

This was a significant test. A camel can drink twenty-five gallons of water in ten minutes, so ten camels would drink two hundred and fifty gallons in ten minutes. How would you like to get two hundred and fifty gallons of water for ten camels? But this is what Eliezar asks of God.

At the beginning of the chapter I mentioned Carrie Sydnor. In her search for a husband, she also put God to the test. She had been praying and she said:

> I want a husband, I'm tried of waiting, so I asked God that I would be involved with this man in 1988, but how did I know this was of God and not just my own idea? I had prayed such things before, and God hadn't done them. I concluded that if we sang a favorite hymn of mine at church, when I go in that morning if they are singing, "Nothing, Absolutely Nothing, Is Impossible With Thee," then that would convince me that God had led me to pray this.

Have you ever done something similar? "God, I need your wisdom. If such-and-such happens, then I know that you are leading me."

Carrie goes on: "The pastor was praying when I arrived late at church. Then everyone stood up and sang, 'Nothing, Absolutely Nothing, Is Impossible With Thee.' I was exultant and anticipated all year what God would do."

This is precisely the strategy of Eliezar. In seeking a spouse and building good relationships, it is imperative that we ask God's will through prayer. As a parent, one of my future worries is the issue of marriage for my children. Seeing marriages fall apart around me gives me great concern about my kids. So I have started praying for their future spouses—providing it is God's will for them to be married. I pray daily for all three of my kids, "God, lead and guide our kids in their dating relationships. God, if it is your will for them to be married, bring the right person into their lives, with the right commitment to Christ." I think as parents we ought to be interceding years and years and years ahead of time for our children in the choices and in the relationships that they make.

Look for Spiritual Qualities in a Spouse

> Before he had finished praying, Rebekah came out with her jar on her shoulder. She was the daughter of Bethuel son of Milcah, who was the wife of Abraham's brother Nahor. The girl was very beautiful, a virgin; no man had ever lain with her. She went down to the spring, filled her jar and came up again.
>
> The servant hurried to meet her and said, "Please give me a little water from your jar."
>
> "Drink, my lord," she said, and quickly lowered the jar to her hands and gave him a drink.
>
> After she had given him a drink, she said, "I'll draw water for your camels too, until they have finished drinking." So she quickly emptied her jar into the trough, ran back to the well to draw more water, and drew enough for all his camels.
>
> Genesis 24:15–20

"Before he had finished praying . . ." This is not coincidence; it is the direction of the Lord. While Eliezar is praying, the answer is already on the way, and her name is Rebekah. She possessed spiritual qualities that are remarkable and necessary for a spiritual relationship.

Purity

"The girl was very beautiful, a virgin; no man had ever lain with her. She went down to the spring, filled her jar and came up again" (Genesis 24:16). She was a virgin—morally pure. This is still a desirable quality in the twentieth century. She did not practice "safe sex." Rather, she practiced "save sex" for marriage. She understood that sex was a gift from God, to be enjoyed within the commitment of heterosexual marriage.

Maybe you are thinking, *That's nice to preach, but I have made those mistakes all ready. What should I do?* First, seek the forgiveness of God. "If we confess our sins, he is faithful and just and will forgive us our sins and to purify us from all unrighteousness" (1 John 1:9). Seek God's forgiveness, and then make a new commitment to God and to the person whom you are dating. Begin practicing God's standard for moral purity.

As a pastor, I have spent a lot of time dealing with couples whose marriages are falling apart. Many times, one of the root problems in the relationship is that prior to the commitment of marriage, they became involved in a physical relationship that was outside the standards of the Word of God. Now they begin to question, *If I was unfaithful to God before marriage, will I now be unfaithful to God within that marriage?*

I understand we live in a sinful world and that we are all sinners. I understand that what I am saying is old-fashioned—not palatable to twentieth-century thinking—but I hold to it because I have seen such suffering. Look for a person to whom you are committing your life, find someone who is willing to live by God's standards and to restrain those physical desires until marriage. Determine before God that, whatever you have done in the past in your relationships, you are going to seek the forgiveness of God, knowing that when God cleanses and sanctifies and justifies, it is as if we had never sinned. Determine before God that your relationship will be within the boundaries of the Word of God.

Humility

> So she quickly emptied her jar into the trough, ran back to the well to draw more water, and drew enough for all his camels. Without saying a word, the man watched her closely to learn whether or not the LORD had made his journey successful.
>
> Genesis 24:20, 21

Notice the descriptions: "Quickly emptied . . . ran back . . . drew enough for all his camels." This speaks of selflessness. Here was someone who set aside her own desires in order to meet the needs of another.

Don't misunderstand the application. I'm not advocating a chauvinistic approach to marriage. "Unless you're willing to fix the car, change the oil, empty the trash, cook the meals, iron the shirts, take care of all of the money, draw 250 gallons of water, you don't belong with me." Now there's a tendency to try to wring that out of the passage. But the real point is that the root of love is a willingness to give up *my* wants, *my* rights, *my* needs for the benefit of the other person.

"For God so loved the world that he gave his one and only Son, that whoever believes in him shall not perish but have eternal life" (John 3:16). What is love? For God so loved the world that he sat up in heaven with an emotional feeling about the world? No! For God so loved the world that *he gave*. And Paul tells us in Ephesians, "Husbands love your wives just as Christ loved the church and *gave* himself up for her."

What should you look for in a life's partner? Someone who demonstrates, not the love you hear about in songs, but rather the love that finds it's root in the Word of God—a love that includes commitment, caring, and giving. A love that says, "I am willing to give of my time and my energy and my resources and my efforts for your benefit and for your good."

If you are in a relationship with an extremely self-centered person, every decision must go her way, whether it's McDonald's or Burger King. If you're in a relationship with someone who is only interested in self, he never offers to help by picking up the dishes or cleaning or pouring coffee. Instead he continually wants you and those around you to serve him. If this is true, then you are in a dangerous relationship.

The root characteristic of love is shown by those willing to set aside their own priorities, their own desires, their own commitments and say to another person, "I love you, and that means I'm committed to you. I am willing to give of myself to meet your needs." Marriage is not a fifty–fifty commitment. It is a 100 percent commitment. It means I give myself 100 percent to my wife, Lorna, and she gives herself to me 100 percent. Whenever there are difficulties in a relationship, they come when someone decides, *I want my way, on my terms, on my schedule.* Not so with the woman who came to the well. She had purity and humility!

Agreement Between Two Families

> Laban and Bethuel answered, "This is from the LORD; we can say nothing to you one way or the other. Here is Rebekah; take her and go, and let her become the wife of your master's son, as the LORD has directed."
>
> Genesis 24:50, 51

Abraham and Rebekah's families had a spiritual unity. This agreement is one of the important things that you ought to look for in a relationship.

Some of you may come from an entire family of nonbelievers. Your parents and siblings are not committed to Christian principles. They may encourage you to marry into a relationship that does not correlate to the principles of Scripture. At that point, you must make your choice on God's principles.

But if both you and the person you plan to marry have godly families, pay careful attention to their concerns and their advice. Look for spiritual unity and agreement between them. In the Old Testament, the families arranged the weddings. (Those of us who have kids entering into their teenage years would probably like to return to that!) That's the way they did it. But in all of that, an underlying principle exists: When you marry that person, you are also building a relationship with his or her family.

The Spiritual Obligations Between Partners

Eliezar brings Rebekah back to Abraham and Isaac.

> Then the servant told Isaac all he had done. Isaac brought her into the tent of his mother Sarah, and he married Rebekah. So she became his wife, and he loved her; and Isaac was comforted after his mother's death.
>
> Genesis 24:66, 67

They met each other's needs. Rebekah became Isaac's wife. He loved her, and she brought comfort to her husband.

Seeking God's Direction

Rebekah and Isaac's story shows God's direction in the events of our daily lives. From it we learn certain key elements of God's direction.

1. He Leads Through Prayer. "Then he prayed, 'O LORD, God of my master Abraham, give me success today, and show kindness to my master Abraham'" (Genesis 24:12).

Are you praying about decisions you need to make regarding relationships? Have you committed them to the Lord? If you need to make a decision in regard to business, have you prayed about it? Recently I talked to some people who attended our church. They drove up from central Ohio and stayed in a hotel overnight. Their mission? To attend Calvary Church on Sunday morning. They had worked at a major company for thirty-one years, and last week, without warning, they were laid off. The man shared, "You will never know what your sermon meant to me this morning. God is at work in those circumstances, and God is at work in my life." What a thing to face! Maybe you're facing significant struggles in life. The road ahead is uncertain. Like Abraham's servant, you face a 450-mile journey to a land where you have never been, to secure a bride you have never seen. Where do you begin? Very simply—on your knees. You start in dependence upon God and seeking his guidance in your life.

2. He Leads Through His Promise. "Then he prayed, 'O Lord, God of my master Abraham, give me success today, and show *kindness* to my master Abraham'" (Genesis 24:12, *italics added*). Notice the word "kindness." It shows us that God keeps his promise. In this verse the servant prays, "God, give me success. And demonstrate your kindness to me." What God promises, he brings to pass. After he reveals Rebekah to Eliezar, the servant worships God:

> Then the man bowed down and worshiped the Lord, saying, "Praise be to the Lord, the God of my master Abraham, who has not abandoned his *kindness* and *faithfulness* to my master. As for me, the Lord has led me on the journey to the house of my master's relatives."
>
> Genesis 24:26, 27, *italics added*

When you face the 450-mile pilgrimage to where you have never been, to seek something you have never seen, and to experience a pathway you've not traveled before, you will discover that God's promises are true. Whenever you face the uncertainty of tomorrow, it's another opportunity to be driven to the Word of God and to the God of the Word. He is the God who always keeps his promise.

3. He Leads with His Presence. Eliezar praises God for his leadership. The New International Version of the Bible states, "the LORD has led me on the journey." I like the King James Version better. "I being in the way, the LORD led me." God led him as he went along in his journey. Eliezar did not take time out to figure out what God wanted. He kept traveling on, and God granted him success along the way.

Do you want to know God's will? You don't bail out. You don't go out into the desert, and say, "Now, Lord, I'm not going to do anything until you show me the way." Obviously at some periods in life we turn to God in prayer and fasting for his direction. But I've discovered that God often meets me as I continue on. As I am in the Word of God, spending time in prayer, sharing my faith, and living for God, he leads me. While I walk in the way, all of a sudden God opens up a path in the desert. God parts the water and gives me direction in my life. Do you know where you are going? Keep reading. Keep praying. Keep believing. Keep walking. Keep serving. Keep praising. Keep singing. Keep going in the way you ought to go, and you will discover his presence.

4. He Leads Us Through Praise. "Then the man bowed down and worshiped the LORD, saying, 'Praise be to the LORD, the God of my master Abraham, who has not abandoned his kindness and faithfulness to my master. As for me, the LORD has led me on the journey to the house of my master's relatives'" (Genesis 24:26, 27).

When I seek God's will in prayer, when I am driven to dependence on his promises, when I discover his presence in my daily walk, then I will be compelled to praise him.

Prayer

I recognize that all of life is making decisions. Help me Lord, to make decisions based on your wisdom and direction. Help me to sense that you lead me all the way. I yield my future to you. Thanks.

Chapter Fifteen

What Matters When You Come to the End of Life?

During the course of a calendar year, I conduct an average of thirty funerals. For many people, the death of a friend or family member is one of the few times when they evaluate their own life and priorities.

When we come to the end of our life here on earth, only two things seem to matter: our relationship to God and our relationship to people. Everything else becomes insignificant. At that time it will not matter how many university degrees we earned or how much money we made or what kind of car we drove. All that matters is God and people.

A Troubling Funeral

The funeral is a bad time to bring up unpleasant things about the deceased. Funerals are funny in a strange sort of way. Few people want to remember the bad times. They praise the deceased and conveniently ignore the bad things their friend did or said. It's unusual, then, to begin the last chapter of Abraham's life with some bad news.

> Abraham took another wife, whose name was Keturah. She
> bore him Zimran, Jokshan, Medan, Midian, Ishbak and Shuah.
> Jokshan was the father of Sheba and Dedan; the descendants of
> Dedan were the Asshumites, the Letushites and the Leummites.
> The sons of Midian were Ephah, Epher, Hanoch, Abida, and
> Eldaah. All these were descendants of Keturah.
>
> Genesis 25:1–4

Abraham had more than one wife. In addition to Sarah, he had
Hagar, who had a son named Ishmael. He also had Keturah,
through whom he had all the people listed in this passage.

Abraham is not the only person in the Old Testament who had
more than one wife. The same is true of Gideon, Saul, David, and
Solomon (who had 700 wives). This raises a troubling question:
Why would Abraham, God's friend, have several wives? Why
would David, a man after God's own heart, have numerous wives?
Why would Solomon, the wisest person who ever lived, have so
many wives?

When I was studying to preach the sermon on the death of
Abraham, I thought *Well, this is tough stuff. I think I will just
ignore it.* On the Friday night of that week, I visited the library
at Calvin College. I was working my way down the periodicals,
picking out what seemed to appeal to me and reading a little bit
here and a little bit there, when I heard someone whisper, "Pastor
Dobson." I turned and saw a young woman who comes to our
church; she is one of those Christians whom I love to be around.
She's excited about God and his Word. She was sitting there reading the Bible.

"I've got a couple of questions," she told me. "You know I've
been reading in the New Testament, and I really like that. I
decided to read the Old Testament. And I'm not sure I like it."

I love honesty. I've thought the same things myself. "Well,
why?" I asked.

"What about all of these people who have several wives?" she questioned.

As a result of that conversation I concluded that I had better deal with the issue in my sermon. Why *did* they do that? People after God's own heart, people committed to God, people walking by faith. Yet for us, in the twentieth century, looking back at their lives, it seems so obvious that they were not living by God's standards.

Keep two important thoughts in mind as I respond to this troubling behavior. First, what Abraham did (having more than one wife) clearly violates the intent of God: "For this reason a man will leave his father and mother and be united to his wife, and they will become one flesh. The man and his wife were both naked, and they felt no shame" (Genesis 2:24, 25).

This is God's standard for marriage: One man plus one woman for one lifetime. What Abraham and Gideon and Saul and David and Solomon and others did was a clear contradiction of God's clearly stated intent for marriage. They disobeyed God.

Second, whenever you disobey God, you will *always* suffer the consequences. This is true of multiple wives. Everyone who violated God's standard in this area of marital faithfulness suffered severe and long-term consequences.

Think for a moment about Abraham's experience. God had promised him a son. Rather than trusting God for the promised child through his wife Sarah, Abraham adopts the ancient practice of taking one of Sarah's servant girls and having a son by her. His name is Ishmael, and he is the head of the Arabs. God finally fulfills his promise through Sarah, and she has a son. His name is Isaac, and he is the father of the Jews. Need I point out that thousands of years later, we are still living with contention, division, hatred, bloodshed, and warfare that has its roots in Abraham's disobedience? Why did he disobey God in this area? It was a common practice in Abraham's day. If you were single or married without children, you were looked down upon in ancient culture. So those who got married and were unable to have children started another option so they could have a family—multiple wives.

Abraham accommodated the truth of God to the generally accepted standards of his culture. The line goes something like this, "Everyone else is doing it. It is accepted by everyone around us. Therefore, there's nothing really wrong with my doing it."

Whenever you violate God's standards and justify your actions on the basis of what everybody else is doing, you head for long-term serious consequences. When it comes to the principles of God's Word, it doesn't matter if the whole world lives in violation. We have a commitment to the transcendent principles of the Word of God. They were valid for Abraham, for Saul, for Gideon, for David, for Solomon, for Paul, for Peter, for John, for Ed Dobson, and for everyone living in the twentieth century. *The standards of God never change.* Abraham violates them and suffers the consequences.

Abraham Remembers His Family

Abraham left everything he owned to Isaac. But while he was still living, he gave gifts to the sons of his concubines and sent them away from his son Isaac to the land of the east.

Altogether, Abraham lived a hundred and seventy-five years. Then Abraham breathed his last and died at a good old age, an old man and full of years; and he was gathered to his people. His sons Isaac and Ishmael buried him in the cave of Machpelah near Mamre, in the field of Ephron son of Zohar the Hittite, the field Abraham had bought from the Hittites. There Abraham was buried with his wife Sarah. After Abraham's death, God blessed his son Isaac, who then lived near Beer Lahai Roi.

Genesis 25:5–11

It is all over for Abraham. At the age of 175 he dies. The text states that he "was gathered to his people." Although it was the end, it was really the beginning. The man who lived by faith died by faith and was gathered with the saints who have gone on before.

What does it mean to die by faith? Let's look at these elements of it.

1. Knowing God Is with You. Dying by faith means you face death with a knowledge of God's presence.

> Even though I walk through the valley of the shadow of death, I will fear no evil, for you are with me; your rod and your staff, they comfort me. You prepare a table before me in the presence of my enemies. You anoint my head with oil; my cup overflows. Surely goodness and love will follow me all the days of my life, and I will dwell in the house of the LORD forever.
>
> Psalm 23:4–6

The God who saved us, the God who strengthens our faith, is the same one who is with us in the valley of the shadow of death.

2. God's Faithful Promise. You can trust his promise. "By faith Abraham, even though he was past age—and Sarah herself was barren—was enabled to become a father because he considered him faithful who had made the promise" (Hebrews 11:11).

These people did not receive the things promised. They saw them at a distance. They were aliens and strangers. Even though Abraham did not see the complete fulfillment of the promise, he still believed God, knowing that beyond his life was the reality of the presence with the Lord.

3. God's Got the Power. You can trust the power of God.

> Listen, I tell you a mystery: We will not all sleep, but we will all be changed—in a flash, in the twinkling of an eye, at the last trumpet. For the trumpet will sound, the dead will be raised imper-

ishable, and we will be changed. For the perishable must clothe
itself with the imperishable, and the mortal with immortality.
When the perishable has been clothed with the imperishable, and
the mortal with immortality, then the saying that is written will
come true: "Death has been swallowed up in victory."

> "Where, O death, is your victory?
> Where, O death, is your sting?"

The sting of death is sin, and the power of sin is the law. But
thanks be to God! He gives us the victory through our Lord Jesus
Christ.

Therefore, my dear brothers, stand firm. Let nothing move you.
Always give yourselves fully to the work of the Lord, because
you know that your labor in the Lord is not in vain.

1 Corinthians 15:51–58

With an awareness of God's presence, God's promise, and
God's power we can face the final reality of death.

> But God will redeem my life from the grave; he will surely
> take me to himself.

Psalm 49:15

> Yet I am always with you; you hold me by my right hand. You
> guide me with your counsel, and afterward you will take me into
> glory. Whom have I in heaven but you? And earth has nothing I
> desire besides you.

Psalm 73:23–25

Prayer

Lord, thank you for faith that sustains us in life and prepares us
for death. Remind me today of what is really important. Grant
that when I die my life will have been spent in useful ways that
will benefit others. May I bring glory to your name as I seek to
follow you.